Thoreau's God

Thoreau's God

Richard Higgins

The University of Chicago Press
Chicago and London

The University of Chicago Press, Chicago 60637
The University of Chicago Press, Ltd., London
© 2024 by The University of Chicago
All rights reserved. No part of this book may be used or reproduced
in any manner whatsoever without written permission, except in
the case of brief quotations in critical articles and reviews. For more
information, contact the University of Chicago Press, 1427 E. 60th St.,
Chicago, IL 60637.
Published 2024
Printed in the United States of America

33 32 31 30 29 28 27 26 25 24   1 2 3 4 5

ISBN-13: 978-0-226-82730-8 (cloth)
ISBN-13: 978-0-226-83645-4 (e-book)
DOI: https://doi.org/10.7208/chicago/9780226836454.001.0001

Library of Congress Cataloging-in-Publication Data

Names: Higgins, Richard, 1952– author.
Title: Thoreau's god / Richard Higgins.
Description: Chicago : The University of Chicago Press, 2024. | Includes
    bibliographical references and index.
Identifiers: LCCN 2024008351 | ISBN 9780226827308 (cloth) |
    ISBN 9780226836454 (ebook)
Subjects: LCSH: Thoreau, Henry David, 1817–1862—Religion.
Classification: LCC PS3057.R4 H54 2024 | DDC 818/.309—dc23/eng/20240317
LC record available at https://lccn.loc.gov/2024008351

♾ This paper meets the requirements of ANSI/NISO Z39.48-1992
(Permanence of Paper).

For Emily, Charlotte, and Nick

I say, God. I am not sure that that is the name. You will know whom I mean.
—THOREAU to Harrison Blake, April 3, 1850

The Almighty is wild above all.
—THOREAU, *Journal*, January 27, 1853

Contents

INTRODUCTION

Thoreau's Religious Quest

Henry David Thoreau was puzzled by the ban a lyceum in New Hampshire placed on the topic of religion in 1856. "How do I know what their religion is," he asked, "and when I am near to or far from it?" It didn't matter, however. When he went ahead and told about the kind of religion he experienced, he wrote after his talk, "the audience never suspected what I was about." One hundred seventy-five years later, we are still having trouble understanding his capacious soul.[1]

Thoreau's religion is first and foremost a riddle, so perhaps that is as it should be. He railed mercilessly at organized religion, calling his Calvinist heritage "an ancient and tottering frame with all its boards blown off." He found its doctrines despairing, its ministers cowardly, its rituals superstitious, and its God impossibly remote yet all controlling. "The church is a sort of hospital for men's souls, and as full of quackery as the hospital for their bodies," he wrote in his first book, *A Week on the Concord and Merrimac Rivers*, published in 1849. "Those who are taken into it live like pensioners in their Retreat or

Sailor's Snug Harbor, where you may see a row of religious cripples sitting outside in sunny weather."[2]

Thoreau's general contrariness and many outright contradictions on the topic—together with his defiant religious pluralism, nature mysticism, and reluctance to utter his innermost religious feelings—have contributed to a consensus that he was "spiritual" in some vague, eclectic way grounded entirely in the natural world and unmoored from common understandings of religion. While that view is not without justification, I think it more likely projects the predominant secularism of our society and of academic studies in particular. I say that because it omits the palpable, undeniable presence of divine mystery in Thoreau's writing. I don't mean in his polemical writings about the errors of organized religion. I mean his sincere and searching remarks about God and his occasional emotional speech *to* God, in his *Journal* and letters.

These are moments when, despite his poison darts, we get a glimpse of that capacious soul. Thoreau was religious to the bone and had a profound sense of the holy. If his views were iconoclastic, his experience of the divine in nature was often rapturous. He disavowed discursive theology, but he spoke of and sought communion with a mystery at the heart of the universe that was at once immanent, or present, in nature and yet transcendent. He called this illimitable presence many names, but he often called it God. Explaining that secret to others was not important. Experiencing it was what mattered. Formal religion with its doctrines, clerics, and creeds was irrelevant to the religion he sought in nature—a "religion by revelation," as Ralph Waldo Emerson called it, or as Thoreau put it, "a newer testament, the Gospel according to this moment." Although Thoreau's religious experience was interior, it gave him a sense of connection with others and informed the moral and political views he expressed through his writings.[3]

A Central Thread

"A man's faith is never contained in his creed," Thoreau wrote in *A Week*. Looking to Thoreau's religious beliefs or affiliation to understand his own faith is like photographing something in insufficient light. The subject is there, but it doesn't come out in the print. Such an angle has led many people to conclude, too hastily, I think, that Thoreau was a solely secular force of nature.[4]

In slighting this deep vein in Thoreau, we miss an essential part of who he was. His religious sensibility was a central thread in his life. It gives depth, context, and greater meaning to his writings. It is woven throughout his scalding critiques of slavery, racism, our materialist culture, and our exploitation of natural resources. It grounds his philosophical views on government and how we relate to the natural world. It gives us a better sense of what motivated him and what he was about. "Without religion or devotion of some kind," he said, "nothing great can be accomplished."[5]

To do better than his lyceum audiences at knowing when Thoreau is talking about religion, we need to look at his lived experience of it. The experiential approach William James took in his classic *Varieties of Religious Experience* helps us do that. For empirical purposes, James defined religion as "the feelings, acts, and experiences of individual men in their solitude, so far as they apprehend themselves to stand in relation to whatever they may consider the divine." He did not dismiss institutional and corporate forms of religion, so important in the history of Western religion; he was simply more interested in people's private encounters with the holy and the difference those moments made in their lives. Today the study of "lived religion" is more inclusive. It looks at more diverse forms of everyday religious practice than did James, who focused on "men in their solitude." Despite such limitations, James is still helpful in looking at Thoreau's religious sensibility and how Thoreau stood in relation to what he considered divine.[6]

Religion for Thoreau was more of an orientation to or attitude about life—one of openness to divine mystery and a desire to draw closer to it. His moments of spiritual exaltation periodically reinforced that quest, but it was his attitude and discipline of faithfulness that sustained him in between such moments. Faithfulness meant more to him than any one faith. Thoreau expressed that devotion in 1853 while walking to Walden by the railroad. The sound of the telegraph wires vibrating in the wooden poles along the track communicated, he thought, a message "from the highest," an "intoxicating" moment of contact "with everlasting truth." He dedicated himself to that truth. "I am pledged to it," he wrote.[7]

Thoreau got a taste of divine mystery in such moments, and a taste was not enough. He wanted to live in a daily abiding awareness of it. Many of us have had such an experience at least once. We cannot explain it, but we know it is true. Thoreau sought to live in fidelity with the spiritual truth as he knew it and to share it with all living things, which he did through his writing and his sympathetic bond with everything in the world around him, from the oldest lichen-covered rock to insects that lived but a day. Thoreau's disavowal of organized religion was thus not a disavowal of the *possibility* of community.

The soul, Emerson said, "never reasons, never proves, it simply perceives." Thoreau's spiritual experience included awe, longing, praise, and gratitude. But above all it was rooted in the kind of direct, unmediated perception to which Emerson alludes. It is the "interior evidence" of the sublime, not the elements or propositions of faith we remember, that convinces us, Thoreau wrote. "It is when we do not have to believe, but come into actual contact with the Truth, and are related to her in the most direct and intimate way."[8]

Helpful also is the work of another scholar, the Romanian historian of religion Mircea Eliade, who took an approach similar to James a half century later. Building on the work of others, Eliade proposed that religion, at its core, involves the experience of the sacred. He held that *homo religious*, the religious person, sees the world in terms of sacred and profane space as well as sacred and profane time. Such a person desires to inhabit the sacred dimension of each sphere and does so through immersion in nature, ritual reenactment, the use of sacred texts and objects, and the cultivation of the religious imagination. Thoreau saw life through such a lens. Walden Pond was his *axis mundi*, the sacred center of his world. He called a swamp his *sanctum sanctorum*, or holy of holies, and a flaming autumn hillside his burning bush. He sought to live within that stratum of deep time that encompasses the primordial dawn of myth and poetry, the eternal now of mysticism, which exists "at the meeting of two eternities, the past and future." Eliade's work is not without controversy, and his phenomenological model again leaves out much, such as communal worship and theological models, but it sheds light on Thoreau's sense of the sacred and his experiential religion in a way that looking at his rejection of the meetinghouse would not.[9]

Fortunately, thanks to a growing receptivity to such approaches, and to the work of scholars like Alan Hodder, David Robinson, Laura Dassow Walls, Lawrence Buell, Christopher

Dustin, Rebecca Kneale Gould, Barry Andrews, Malcolm Clemens Young, Alda Balthrop-Lewis, and Lydia Willsky-Ciollo, among others, the long neglect of Thoreau's spirituality has begun to shift in the last two decades. The publication in 2004 of Thoreau's esoteric but spiritually revealing epistles to his Worcester friend and disciple Harrison Gray Otis Blake, *Letters to a Spiritual Seeker*, have also helped bring Thoreau's religiosity to the fore.

"A Fresh, Simple Life with God"

It is remarkable how many of Thoreau's contemporaries recognized this deep vein in his character. John Weiss, a Unitarian minister and Thoreau's Harvard classmate, called him a "pure soul" on a par with the Puritan divine Jonathan Edwards. "No writer of the present day is more religious," Weiss wrote, or "more profoundly penetrated with the redeeming power of simple integrity, and the spiritualizing effect of a personal consciousness of God." Blake, a Unitarian minister who met Thoreau at Emerson's house in 1844 and was impressed early on by his spiritual gravitas, wrote in his first letter to him, in 1848, "If I understand rightly the significance of your life, this is it: You would sunder yourself from society . . . that you may lead a fresh, simple life with God. Instead of breathing new life into old forms, you would have a new life without and within." Emerson said that despite Thoreau's penchant for "a certain petulance of remark in reference to churches or churchmen," he "was a person of a rare, tender, and absolute religion, a person incapable of any profanation, by act or by thought." Few know as much about nature's secrets as Thoreau did, Emerson said, and "none in a more large and religious synthesis."[10]

Thoreau's close friends, including Bronson Alcott and

Ellery Channing, commented on this quality in him, as did his acquaintance and early biographer Franklin Sanborn, who called Thoreau "deeply religious" despite his scorn for conventional faiths. Maria Bridge Pratt, the wife of Thoreau's friend and fellow botanizer Minot Pratt, frequently saw him at their house. "Yes, he was religious," she wrote. "He was more like the ministers and others, that is, like what they would wish and try to be." A year after his death, Thoreau's sister Sophia gently criticized Emerson's dour portrayal of her brother in his eulogy. "I think Henry was a person of much more faith than Mr. Emerson," she wrote a friend. Emily Lyman of Philadelphia, who was born in 1845, never met Thoreau, but after reading his journals, which were first published in the 1880s, she became an ardent devotee. She was led around Thoreau's haunts in Concord by Alfred Hosmer, an amateur photographer and early Thoreau enthusiast.[11]

> I suppose that I should surprise most persons were I to say that it is the religious side of Thoreau's character that interests me deeply, for religious I believe he was, in a true and high sense of the word. I care not that he launched forth invectives against the preachers and church organizations— some of them probably deserved it. . . . He was not only "self-centered," he was God-centered. . . . I believe that his beautiful, pure life was the direct outcome of his faith. He drew his inspiration from the highest source.[12]

Thoreau's spiritual depth was also evident to Herbert Wendell Gleason, one of America's great landscape photographers. From 1899 to 1930, Gleason returned over and over to Concord, taking thousands of pictures of Thoreau's favorite natural scenes to create a visual archive of his world. "Nothing more deeply impresses itself upon the mind of one who reads Thoreau's *Journal* sympathetically," Gleason wrote in 1917, "than the conviction that Thoreau possessed a profoundly religious nature."[13]

Emerson's praise in his eulogy at Thoreau's funeral, on May 9, 1862, was mixed with harsher words. But whatever faults of temperament Thoreau possessed, Emerson said, "he was not disobedient to the heavenly vision."

Blazing a Trail for Seekers

Although Thoreau's spiritual quest was a personal one, he did not keep it to himself. Emulating Goethe's vocation "faithfully to describe what he sees," Thoreau devoted his life to communicating his vision. His writings and the example of his life helped blaze a trail that many others have traveled. "Fifty years from now," he predicted in 1850, "the majority of people will believe as I do now." Thoreau was off by a century, and by how many might share his beliefs, but his audacious prophecy was remarkably prescient. Spiritual seekers today are discovering a chord of recognition in Thoreau's eclectic, experiential, and noninstitutional spirituality. He appeals to people who are looking, as the late great nature writer Barry Lopez wrote, "for anyone who could speak the language of the god of no particular religion." This is not because Thoreau's religious views are being newly discovered, but because American culture has come round to embrace them. Indeed, Thoreau's religious naturalism may help explain why he has more readers today than any American author from before the Civil War.[14]

Pierre Teilhard de Chardin, the French Jesuit scientist and theologian, once said we are not human beings on a spiritual journey but rather spiritual beings on a human journey. Thoreau, whose spiritual aspirations were firmly grounded in the earth, was as much simultaneously a spiritual and a human being as anyone of whom I can think. That is why he is seen today as a credible guide to the spiritual life.[15]

Thoreau helped expand the category of religion in his day. But he stands in a long line of liberalizing reformers—from proto-Protestant forerunners, such as Peter Waldo, John Wycliffe, and Jan Hus, to the Quaker mystic George Fox and antinomian Puritans, such as Anne Hutchinson, who placed the indwelling spirit of God above the Law of Moses, to the nature Romanticism of Wordsworth, Goethe, and Coleridge, and his fellow Transcendentalists, especially Emerson, and, indirectly, Friedrich Schleiermacher—all of whom sought a truer, more interior form of religion. Thoreau's spirituality also has to be situated within the protean religious liberalism of the nineteenth century, a major cultural force that included not only Unitarians and Transcendentalists but also Quakers, Reform Jews, Free Religion thinkers, Theosophists, and advocates of Asian religious practices. Religious liberalism tended to combine social action and political engagement with a mystical, interior search for truth and an emphasis on self-expression. Thoreau's religion synthesized both aspects, although today's spiritual seekers tend to find more inspiration in the latter. In essence, the fluid, fractious, and dynamic religious culture of Thoreau's day continues to upend and redefine American religion today.[16]

Thoreau was a voracious reader, and his religious thought bears lesser or greater relation to his forebears and fellow freethinkers, but he mostly formulated his religion from his own experience. If he has greater influence today than those forebears and peers, it is because he articulated that liberal religious vision with an originality, courage, clarity, sincerity, vividness, and beauty that few have.

Clues to the Riddle

It is for these reasons that I see Thoreau's God as a riddle, rather than as the oxymoron many people have taken it to be. Given the head-scratching things Thoreau said about religion, his refusal to be linked with any one form of it, and the dissonance between his righteous pronouncements and his private experience, a riddle may be just what Thoreau intended. If so, Thoreau's writings, including his *Journal*, his correspondence (especially his letters to Harrison Blake), *A Week on the Concord and Merrimack Rivers*, *Walden*, and his social reform and natural history essays, contain clues to help us try to put the pieces of the puzzle together.

This book explores facets of and questions about Thoreau's religiosity roughly in the order of his writings. Drawing on his early *Journal* and poems, the first four chapters explore Thoreau's core sense of reverence, his understanding of religion as a way of living, his sense of wonder at the beauty and harmony of nature, and his profound interior experience of sacred mystery. These chapters also look at some of the early influences that shaped his religious sensibility, including Transcendentalism, the religious naturalism of Romantic thinkers and poets, and Hindu and Chinese scriptures. Thoreau was also indelibly stamped by his Christian upbringing.

The next two chapters, "A Puritan Golden Calf" and "Rejecting Repentance," look at the religious impulse behind Thoreau's harsh invective against institutional religion in *A Week*. Thoreau left the meetinghouse as a young man not because it stood for religion but because it profaned it. Behind his criticism was a desire to commune with the divine.

Chapters 7 through 10 explore Thoreau's mystical experience in nature, his reflections on the source of nature's divinity, and his nonsystematic theology. Thoreau held no fixed position but located a reality and source of transcendence beyond himself. His theism was contingent, fluid, and never final, more of a fleeting glance into the depths. His God was an infinite, wild, life-giving presence manifest in the natural world and yet not contained by it. At the same time, Thoreau was ambivalent about the word *God*. He insisted on God's ineffability; paradoxically, though, as a literary artist he used personal and figurative terms to portray God as the ultimate creative force within and beyond nature.

Chapters 11 and 12 address the relational dimension of Thoreau's theology and his ambivalent relationship to, and striking silence about, Jesus. Thoreau could not accept the suffering, redemptive, and divine figure of Christian dogma, but he found moral inspiration in Jesus's uncompromising message of justice and love.

In chapters 13 and 14, I consider how Thoreau used religious language to reclaim the sacred from formal religion and reframe it for his readers. He refused to allow organized religion to have the last say about God. Biblical imagery and syntax form a hidden stream in his prose. *Walden*, his modern-day scripture, offers a fundamentally religious vision of our relationship to nature. More than mere literary flourishes, Thoreau's religious wordplay in his masterpiece conveyed what true religion meant to him.

The next two chapters, "'I Hear the Unspeakable'" and "'A Place beyond All Place,'" explore the spiritual resonance silence held for Thoreau and the down-to-earth mysticism of his late natural history studies. Thoreau felt that a true religious feeling is not spoken. Silence held a deeply spiritual quality for him. And the "distant shore," "other world," and "another realm" that Thoreau often mentioned in his more mystical mode turns out to be a world within this present one that we assume we know so well. In the last decade of his life, his materialism became his mysticism. The book concludes with chapter 17, "Thoreau's Refining Fire," about the reformational zeal and the role of love in Thoreau's religion.

Obstacles

As with any puzzle, there are challenges. The first is the inherent subjectivity of my topic, which makes this book only one interpretation. Thoreau's religious thought also defies too direct and literal an approach. We must not rudely probe any sanctuary of life, he reminded us, or we shall find only surface. "The ultimate expression or fruit of any created thing is a fine effluence which only the most ingenuous worshipper perceives at a reverent distance from its surface even."[17]

Thoreau's views on religion shift with his rhetorical purpose or mood, expostulating for dramatic effect here and baring his soul there. He wove deceptive and subtle caveats into his remarks that subvert his apparent meaning. His love of wordplay is another factor. After hoeing beans at Walden one day, Thoreau joined a luckless fisherman "who had been fishing on the pond since morning, as silent and motionless as a duck or a floating leaf." Thoreau, "after practicing various kinds of philosophy," decided the man "belonged to the ancient sect of Coenobites," or monks who live in a community, as opposed to eremitic monks or hermits. But it's more likely Thoreau was himself fishing for a pun, and the man belonged to that sect of fishermen who *see no bites*. Confounding matters, Thoreau's views are inconsistent, befitting his dialectical and idiosyncratic approach to religion, now tacking to the ideal or neo-Platonic side of the river, now back to the more empirical bank.[18]

Then there is his strange privacy. Thoreau has to be among the least self-revealing individuals who ever poured their lives into a nearly two-million-word journal. He was very particular about what he shared, and when it came to his health, his sexuality, his grief, and his bouts of "melancholy," he often omitted the particular altogether. One looks in vain for more than a veiled allusion to the death of his brother, John, one of the central events of his life. In the *second* half of *A Week*, which is dedicated to John, Thoreau finally speaks personally of his brother, his actual companion on the river trip, who hovers indistinctly over the narrative. "My Friend is not of some other race or family of men, but flesh of my flesh, bone of my bone," he writes with almost shocking pathos. "He is my real brother." After Thoreau was fitted for false teeth at 34, he mused eloquently about taking ether for the extraction—but did not mention that his teeth had rotted and must have hurt. He was equally vague or silent about the tubercular bouts and other mysterious illnesses that plagued him, and about much else in his personal life.[19]

God is also beyond rational thought for Thoreau. In this he is allied with the mystical tradition known as the *via negativa*, or apophatic theology. *Apophatic* is from the Greek for "no speech" and refers to the belief that, despite our innate capacity to know God intuitively, no quality or attribute of God can be posited with confidence. What mattered to Thoreau was the music behind a religious feeling, not the lyrics. "Give me a sentence which no intelligence can understand," he wrote about the Hindu scriptures. "There must be a kind of life and palpitation to it, and under its words a kind of blood must circulate forever."[20]

His Life as a Prayer

The biggest problem may be what it means to call Thoreau religious, given his antipathy to institutional religion or fixed beliefs. One could point to his simple, ascetic lifestyle, which Alda Balthrop-Lewis presents as a religiously informed practice of political dissent; his reclamation of ancient wisdom from the world's religions; or his sometimes strident philosophical views on the topic. What makes him religious even more in my view are certain attitudes or habits of mind and heart he possessed—those of reverence, devotion, aspiration to a higher life, disciplined attention, awe, gratitude, and subordination to something larger than himself. In essence, Thoreau's whole life was a prayer.[21]

Thoreau had a fundamental reverence for the holiness and benevolence of creation. "I would fain improve every opportunity to wonder and worship, as a sunflower welcomes the light," he wrote in 1856. "The more thrilling, wonderful, divine objects I behold in a day, the more expanded and immortal I become."[22]

Thoreau once told his friend Blake that, while he saw no reason to congratulate himself on his actual life, "for my faith and aspiration I have respect. It is from these that I speak." It is also from those qualities that I have tried to let Thoreau speak in this book. The great Jewish mystic and theologian Abraham Joshua Heschel captured this side of Thoreau when he wrote, "To pray is to take notice of the wonder, to regain a sense of the mystery that animates all beings, the divine margin in all attainments. Prayer is our humble answer to the inconceivable surprise of living."[23]

ONE

An Offering to the Gods

On Wednesday, January 6, 1841, an independent-minded 23-year-old man strode down Concord's snow-covered streets to the Town House and gave a one-sentence note on a half-sheet of light brown paper to the town clerk, Cyrus Stow. Its cursive letters were firm and sweeping, especially the large first one. "I do not wish to be considered a member of the First Parish in this town." It was signed "Henry D. Thoreau."[1]

The note has been called Thoreau's "resignation" from First Parish in Concord, the Unitarian congregation founded by the town's Puritan settlers, but that is not quite correct. Thoreau was careful not to admit that he ever belonged, as he would explain years later in his essay "Resistance to Civil Government," better known as "Civil Disobedience." Fudging the truth slightly, he wrote in 1849 that in order to avoid being taxed to support the minister, "I condescended to make some such statement as this in writing: 'Know all men by these presents, that I, Henry Thoreau, do not wish to be regarded as a member of any incorporated society I have not joined.'" Concord's religious Robespierre would not even name the "incorporated society" to which he did not belong as the church in which he was baptized and catechized.[2]

Thoreau's feistiness aside, the larger point is that he was neither rejecting religion nor even, as he saw it, giving up a religious affiliation. He just preferred the one he had in the woods. The soil of conventional religion was too thin in which to grow his soul.

Thoreau was often irreverent, but he was never irreligious— if by *religious* one does not mean institutional, creedal, or ritual religion, but the profound interior experience of a sacred mystery that is greater than ourselves. If by *religion* we mean awe at the miracle that we dwell in a universe we have not made or the recognition that we are finite beings who depend on the infinite. Or if we use the wonderful short definition of religion from the comparative religion scholar Diana Eck: the urge to bow and remove our shoes. By those measures, Thoreau was incurably religious. He had a sincere faith in the ultimate goodness of nature as a divine creation. His ideas about religion changed throughout his life, but his core reverence was the vestal fire of the temple, "which is never permitted to go out, but burns steadily, and with as pure a flame, on the obscure provincial altar, as in Numa's temple at Rome."[3]

A Seeker's Journal

In January 1841, Thoreau was a young Transcendentalist and aspiring writer on the brink. Notwithstanding his performative brush-off of his family church, his private *Journal* for that month shows a man actively seeking to find the divine in nature and to fathom its depths.

On January 2, he imagined that the bitter winds of winter drove away all falsity and "contagion" from the landscape, leaving only what God originally created. "At such times it seems as if all God's creatures were called in for shelter, and what stayed out must be part of the original frame of the universe—and of such valor as God himself," he wrote.

On January 4, he saw the natural world as the soil of the soul. Personifying nature as a woman, he wrote of knowing one "who is as true to me and as incessant with her mild rebuke as the blue sky." Her wind and rain wash off all pretension and taint. "Her eyes are such bottomless and inexhaustible depths as if they were the windows of nature, through which I caught glimpses of the native land of the soul."

On January 13, Thoreau imagined his "garret"—the cramped attic in the family home on what is now the site of the Concord Free Public Library—as a kind of monastic scriptorium in which to make offerings to heaven with his pen. He figuratively depicted his manuscripts as palimpsests (a writing medium, such as vellum or parchment, that has been scraped clean for reuse but which contains a hidden layer of words visible only to the keenest eye). Thoreau speculated that only a "godlike insight" could read the hidden text in his words—a daunting and humbling warning to any who would seek to glimpse his soul.

We should offer up our *perfect* thoughts to the gods daily. Our writing should be hymns and psalms. Who keeps a journal is a purveyor [provider] for the Gods. There are two sides to every sentence; the one is contiguous to me, but the other faces the gods, and no man ever fronted it. When I utter a thought I launch a vessel which never sails in my haven more, but goes sheer off into the deep. Consequently it demands a godlike insight, a fronting view, to read what was greatly written.

(Curiously, eleven years later, Thoreau wrote again about ideas that soar above us, one side turned toward the heavens and one toward the earth. Others may consider such a notion "moonshine," but for himself, he wrote, "I will be thankful that I see so much as one side of a celestial idea, one side of the rainbow and the sunset sky, the face of God alone."[4])

On January 25, 1841, Thoreau compared himself to a bird fluttering restlessly on a branch in the fall as it prepares to migrate to a warmer clime. His whole body, he wrote, anticipated the breaking up of winter with a "migratory instinct."

> This indefinite restlessness and fluttering on the perch do, no doubt, prophesy the final migration of souls out of nature to a serene summer, in long harrows and waving lines in the spring weather, over what fair uplands and fertile Elysian meadows winging their way at evening and seeking a resting-place with loud cackling and uproar!

Thoreau left the meetinghouse, in short, not because it stood for religion, but because it profaned the truer kind of religion he found in nature. "We check and repress the divinity that stirs within us and fall down and worship the divinity that is dead without us," he wrote in 1851. Nine years later, he held the same view. It is only the dead husk of Christianity that men run after and revere, he said. "The kernel is still the very least and rarest of all things."[5]

A Turning Point

As the tone of his note suggests, the young man who strolled down to the clerk's office in January 1841 was confident in his views. There had been more promise than bankable accomplishments in the four years since he left Harvard; still, he had become the protégé of the lion of American letters, Ralph Waldo Emerson. And with his first poems, essays, and translations coming out in the *Dial*, he still had high hopes for a literary career.

Events and developments in the coming months and years, however, would dent that confidence and alter his religious outlook.

On April 1, 1841, the declining health of his beloved brother, John, who was already showing signs of consumption, forced the closure of the school they ran and precipitated a vocational crisis Thoreau would struggle with until undertaking his experiment at Walden. A few weeks later, Thoreau moved into Emerson's house, where he read the first English translations of the ancient scriptures of India and China. The spiritual truths in them, and especially their proclamation of the divinity in the human soul, moved Thoreau and confirmed his emerging belief that religion was about unity, not division. His reading in Eastern religion also cast Christianity in a more equivocal light by comparison, demonstrating it to be but one of the world's religious mythologies.

On January 11, 1842, Thoreau was shattered by John's death from tetanus. It was an assault on his own vital force, and it challenged his faith in life and understanding of God. Thoreau would emerge from the shock, grief, and depression with a literally budding faith in the immortality of nature. He came to see that individuals die, but nature lives on. Eight weeks after John's death he could write Emerson, if with more bravery than belief, "Every blade in the field—every leaf in the forest—lays down its life in its season as beautifully as it was taken up. It is the pastime of a full quarter of the year. Dead trees, sere leaves, dried grass and herbs—are not these a good part of our life?" In his grief Thoreau began moving toward his mature view of death as a portal of transformation. Seen as an accident or rupture, death is tragic, he said; but seen as a natural law, it is beautiful.[6]

Even in the early 1840s, it was dawning on Thoreau that his relationship with Emerson might not lead to the intimacy he so craved. "My friend is cold and reserved because his love for me is waxing and not waning," Thoreau wrote on March 20, 1842, one of many times over the next decade that he would bemoan the cooling of their bond.[7]

As the 1840s progressed, Thoreau would mostly resolve these challenges. He would triumphantly work out in *Walden* the question of how to live, and make a living, while remaining faithful to one's genius. After a period of rebellion, he would integrate his understanding of Eastern religion into his eclectic faith without shedding elements of his Puritan heritage. And he would turn John's death into an impetus to live fully and savor the gift of nature, as if for both of them.

Only his rupture with Emerson, which would lead Thoreau to an extremely idealized view of friendship—even to the point of viewing God as a benign, mysterious friend—remained a lifelong hurt.

TWO

The Shaping of a Seeker

Two stories are told about Thoreau as a toddler. In one, his mother, Cynthia, asked him why he lay awake at night while his brother slept soundly in their common bed, according to Edward Waldo Emerson. "I've been looking through the stars to see if I could see God behind them," the 3- or 4-year-old Thoreau replied. And Franklin Sanborn, in his biography, reports that one winter while out sledding, Thoreau's playmates chided him that his sled was worthless because its runners were wood, not iron. Upon coming home, Thoreau said he did not want to die and go to heaven if it was too grand a place for his meager sled.[1]

Neither story may be factual, but both have the ring of truth. Thirty years later, Thoreau would pronounce it his profession to find God in nature and not just in the clouds. And although he depicted heaven figuratively hundreds of times in his *Journal*, he wanted no part of any heaven too good for wood or disconnected from the earth in any way.

Thoreau was a born seeker. He had an inherent sense of reverence and, if one reads him carefully, humility, at least regarding the divine, before which he fell silent. He also bowed before nature's mysteries: the trees, he said, point to a place beyond where our feet cannot take us. His keen and searching awareness of a hidden, numinous dimension of reality, along with the religious liberalism and idealism he developed at Harvard and as a member of Concord's Transcendentalist circle, inclined him toward a spiritual outlook on life. Thoreau saw the world as either sacred or profane, and he desired as much as possible to live in the former and eschew the latter. "Those divine sounds," he wrote, "which are uttered to our inward ear—which are breathed in with the zephyr or are reflected from the lake—come to us noiselessly, bathing the temples of the soul, as we stand motionless amid the rocks."[2]

Concord's Holy Wars

The anti-Calvinist spirit of Thoreau's day, which led to the Unitarian–Trinitarian split during his childhood, his reverence for the natural world, his mentorship under Emerson, his exposure to Unitarian theology at Harvard, and his bond with other Transcendentalists all directly influenced Thoreau's emerging religious sensibility. The splintering of the New England church in the early nineteenth century hastened a movement in America toward religious affiliation by volition rather than by birth, for which Thoreau, with others, would provide a sound rationale. (That trend continues unabated to this day, with the twist that a growing number of spiritually inclined Americans are opting for no affiliation at all.)

Thoreau was born in 1817 into a world of swift change. Opposing movements sought to fill the void created by the decline of Massachusetts's Congregational Standing Order, which gave state sanction to the churches founded by the Puritans. Many of those old churches, especially in and around Boston, had gradually embraced a nascent Unitarianism by 1800, moving toward a more loving God and a more positive view of human nature. The Unitarian churches in eastern Massachusetts were soon facing infighting on two fronts. First, in the 1820s, traditionalists opposed to their liberal bent began leaving them to form their own Trinitarian (Congregational) churches. Then, in the 1830s, Transcendentalists of the opposite persuasion drifted away to create a form of non-sectarian religion—Theodore Parker called it "absolute, pure Morality; absolute pure Religion; the love of God acting without let or hindrance"—beyond institutional walls, creeds, and clerics. Meanwhile, other sects were proliferating amid the religious fervor of Second Great Awakening during the early nineteenth century.[3]

Home, then, was the locus of religion, and there Thoreau was surrounded by God-fearing Calvinist relatives. Both of his grandmothers, Rebecca Thoreau and Mary Dunbar; three of his maiden aunts, Elizabeth, Jane, and Maria Thoreau; and his mother, Cynthia, all made public professions of faith in Concord in the years leading up to Thoreau's birth.[4]

Cynthia and the aunts wanted a sterner faith than they found at First Parish, where Thoreau was baptized in 1817, and which under Ezra Ripley's sixty-three-year pastorate had gradually liberalized. In 1826, the three aunts were among nine disgruntled conservatives who, much to Ripley's chagrin, rose from their pews and walked a few steps across the brook behind First Parish to start a new Trinitarian church. In April 1827, Cynthia followed, intending to join. Later, Cynthia's brother, Charles, and her sister Louisa would join the dissidents. Over the next year, and while the startup church's new minister, Daniel Southmayd, and his wife were boarding in her home, Cynthia began questioning a central point of faith in the new church's creed: Did she worship Jesus fully as Jesus Christ, as God manifest in human flesh, or was Jesus a mediator or sacred being drawn from, but ultimately lesser than, God? The historian Robert Gross has documented that Joanna Southmayd warned Cynthia about her "pride of reasoning." (If there is a gene for such pride, Henry certainly inherited it.) In the end, Cynthia decided she could not in good conscience accept the divinity of Jesus nor assent to the creed. Despite pressure, she bravely returned to First Parish, effectively splitting the family. One can only imagine the diverse religious views 10-year-old Henry heard around the house. Cynthia's principled decision to follow her conscience—a stance her son would later describe as a "majority of one"— almost surely made an impression on Thoreau, and it seems probable that the internecine squabbling over doctrine contributed to his dismissal of organized religion.[5]

Amid all this, Thoreau was marinated in religion, though not always to the intended effect. His confinement indoors on the Sabbath turned him strongly against "sedentary" religion. "When I was young and compelled to pass my Sunday in the house without the aid of interesting books," he recalled at 35, "I used to spend many an hour till the wished-for sundown, watching the martins soar, from an attic window; and fortunate indeed did I deem myself when a hawk appeared in the heavens . . . and I searched for hours till I had found his mate. They, at least, took my thoughts from earthly things."[6]

Thoreau attended "Sabbath School," which began formally at First Parish the year after he was born, where he studied the Bible with about 120 other young "scholars" (boys and girls). Thoreau gained acquaintance with Scripture, but otherwise the attempt to train the independent-minded boy in the faith did not go well for Christianity. As an adult, Thoreau quipped that he was at times "slightly prejudiced" against the

New Testament because the life of Jesus had been edited by
Christians. Such sarcasm conceals the fact that one thing he
did gain from being raised in a devout Christian home and attending Sabbath school, as well as his later study of the Bible
in Greek at Harvard, was a bone-bred knowledge and love of
the magisterial poetics of the King James Bible. Few American authors can match him in the frequency of his direct allusions to biblical passages.[7]

Transcendental Apprentice

By the time Thoreau arrived at Harvard in 1833, the college
had already moved beyond its Calvinist roots to embrace a
rational Unitarianism. Although Harvard continued to rely on
the authority of the Bible and to justify the miracles of the
Gospels as a grounds for faith (which the Transcendentalists
would soon reject), it emphasized a more loving God; the
goodness and potential of human nature, rather than its depravity; New Testament ethics; and the right to interpret the
Bible according to one's individual conscience. Thoreau was
also exposed at Harvard to Scottish commonsense realism,
which, in contrast to the sense-based empiricism of Locke,
argued for the existence of innate ideas and the mind's ability
to perceive them intuitively. Thoreau would develop that view
when he appealed to a higher law in "Civil Disobedience."

There comes a time in most people's lives, especially
young, impressionable people, when they are especially open
to the influence of others. Thoreau had two such moments
in college. In late 1835 and early 1836, he was initiated into
Transcendentalism as the movement was coming together
when he took the equivalent of a work-study break to teach
school for six weeks in Canton, Massachusetts. There he lived
with the fiery Orestes Brownson, a self-taught rural Unitarian

minister and important early Transcendentalist. Brownson was then writing his groundbreaking *New Views of Society, Christianity, and the Church* (1836) which sought to distinguish religion from religious institutions, called for radical social equality, and preached a "doctrine of atonement" that sought to unite spirit and matter. (To make his point, Brownson styled this union of heaven and earth "at-one-ment.") It was Thoreau's first encounter with a firebrand intellectual and social justice crusader, and the experience had a lasting impact on him.[8]

The second and even more powerful moment came a year later when he read *Nature*, Emerson's 1836 manifesto of Transcendentalism. Thoreau checked out the book in the spring of his junior year and again in the fall of his senior year, and was enthralled by its call to know the divine through direct experience and by its view of nature as an organic language of spirit. It struck Thoreau with a force like no other book in his life, except possibly the ancient Hindu text *Laws of Manu*, which he would swoon over in 1841. *Nature*'s influence is evident in a graceful riff of pure idealism Thoreau wrote in 1840, about the reflections of trees on water, that he would weave into his first book, *A Week on the Concord and Merrimack Rivers.*

> For every oak and birch too growing on the hill-top, as
> well as for these elms and willows, we knew that there was
> a graceful ethereal and ideal tree making down from the
> roots, and sometimes Nature in high tides brings her mirror
> to its foot and makes it visible. The stillness was intense and
> almost conscious, as if it were a natural Sabbath, and we
> fancied that the morning was the evening of a celestial day.[9]

Thoreau would later diverge from Emerson's pure idealism, but he never shed his appreciation of the symbolic value of nature, nor would he cease to insist on direct experience of the divine. In 1838, Emerson gave Thoreau a second jolt of inspiration with his Divinity School Address, which jettisoned the underpinnings of historical Christianity in favor of the indwelling divinity in the human soul and faith in its capacity to intuitively grasp the spiritual and moral laws in nature. Emerson's suggestion to know God "without mediator or veil" became for Thoreau a lifelong imperative. Emerson was drawing on and deepening Thoreau's indirect acquaintance with the radical views of the German theologian Friedrich Schleiermacher, who believed religion is founded on interior feeling, not on the doctrines or authority of the church. Schleiermacher put the inward and essential before the outward and accidental, as Thoreau would do in *A Week*.

Schleiermacher held that religion consists of a feeling of reliance on God as the source of our being, as opposed to formal religious ideas or behavior. He is traditionally quoted as referring to "a feeling of absolute dependence on God," but scholars have recently argued that a more accurate translation from the nineteenth-century German is an "*absolute feeling* of dependence on God." In our therapeutic American culture, the word *dependent* has a negative shading. A million self-help books, phone apps, podcasts, and videos urge us to be self-reliant individuals. "Codependency" is a sign of a sick mind. But to Schleiermacher, the reality and immediacy of our intuition that we depend on a power greater than ourselves is the very wellspring of religion. It is the recognition that as finite, mortal beings, we pale before the infinite—that the humility to kneel before this higher power gives us the inner power to stand to our full height.

Despite the similarity in the two men's views, there is no evidence that Thoreau read Schleiermacher. Rather, he seems to have picked up the German's outlook by Transcendentalist osmosis. Thoreau did not want to study religion; he wanted to experience it. In marked contrast to his study of science, he rarely cited spiritual teachers and theologians. He did sometimes refer to primary texts but rarely to their interpreters.[10]

A year after the Divinity School Address, Thoreau put his Transcendentalist apprenticeship into practice when he declined to attend church with a girl he loved. When 18-year-old Ellen Sewell, the niece of a boarder in Thoreau's house and daughter of a conservative Unitarian minister, visited Concord that summer, Thoreau was, for perhaps the only time in his life, deeply smitten. He took her sailing, wrote her moony poems, and carved their initials on a wooden bridge. He would eventually propose to her. But when Ellen asked him to go to church with her that July, Thoreau declined. He told her that he worshipped outdoors. Thoreau was as good as his word. On January 30, 1841, for example, he was out after a snowstorm. Pines bowed over by snow formed arched aisles in the wood, and light poured dimly through their branches, "as through windows of ground glass," suggesting stained glass windows. "You glance up these paths," he wrote, "closely embowered by bent trees, as through the side aisles of a cathedral, and expected to hear a choir chanting from their depths."[11]

Sanskrit "in My Brain"

Another influence was Greek myth and religion, to which Thoreau developed a lifelong devotion while at Harvard. It appealed to him because its gods were more human, fallible, approachable, and in touch with nature, and because it nurtured his mythological view of the world. He was also influenced by the Hindu scriptures and Confucian thought, which form an important thread in both *A Week* and *Walden*. The Vedic scriptures possessed a sublimity and pure consciousness of soul that appealed to Thoreau, but without the miracles and self-mortification of Christianity that he found offensive. In them Thoreau found a dedication to the realm of spirit over matter and an emphasis on devotion and self-mastery that helped shape his perennial philosophy. They also showed him that if Christianity had a monopoly on worship in his New England, it had none on the truth.

James Russell Lowell mocked Thoreau's digressive dives into Eastern religion in *A Week*. "What," he asked, "have the Concord and Merrimack to do with Boodh?" But Thoreau's attraction to Eastern thought was sincere and profound, if selective and based on the first translations that emerged in the late 1700s as a result of trade with India and China. "I cannot read a sentence in the book of the Hindoos without being elevated as upon the table-land of the Ghats," Thoreau wrote in 1841, referring to a mountainous plateau in southern India. And: "In the Hindoo scripture the idea of man is quite illimitable and sublime. There is nowhere a loftier conception of his destiny." A year later he declared, "In my brain is the sanscrit [Sanskrit] which contains the history of the primitive times."[12]

Thoreau was especially entranced by the *Institutes of Hindu Law* (*Manusmṛiti*), or the *Laws of Manu*, as they are known—a set of sacred legal texts concerning the creation of the world and the laws of karma, rebirth, and liberation. The work strengthened his idealism and shaped his view of the soul. He also published extracts from it in a column he edited, "Ethnical Scriptures," in the Transcendentalist journal the *Dial*, including "The resignation of all pleasures is far better than the attainment of them" and "The hand of the artist employed in his art is always pure." Thoreau wrote in his *Journal* on May 31, 1841, "The laws of Menu are the laws of you and me, and no more to be refuted than the wind." (Thoreau spelled the work *Menu*, following Sir William Jones's 1796 translation.)

Around this time, Thoreau also read an early edition of the Buddhist Lotus Sutra in French, and he took notes on the Chinese Four Books, which introduced the fundamentals of Confucianism. The Bhagavad Gita arrived in Concord in 1845. Thoreau read it, was deeply impressed, and carried a copy to Walden. He included a chapter on its timeless and exalted qualities (and those of the *Laws of Manu*) in *A Week*, and in *Walden* he mused that ice harvested from the pond for export might find its way to India, where water from Walden might mingle with that of the sacred Ganges.

The nature piety and Romanticism of Goethe and Coleridge, and especially of Wordsworth, were also strong influences on Thoreau's religion of the 1830s and '40s. Thoreau's accounts of ecstatic spiritual experience were often tinged with an elegiac sense of loss that, as Alan Hodder has shown, bear a powerful echo of Wordsworth's belief that poetry is "the spontaneous overflow" of powerful emotions "recollected in tranquility." Like the English poet, Thoreau pined for "authentic tidings of invisible things," and in his early work he dipped his pen in Wordsworth's inkwell.[13]

Although it was not a direct influence on him, Thoreau also stands in a long line of mystics who practiced the *via negativa* (negative way)—the belief that God is outside humanity's logical perception or grasp and can be known only through a kind of blind groping in faith. And he stands in an equally long line of divines who found spiritual solace in the "book of nature," from St. Francis to Thoreau's Puritan forebear Jonathan Edwards. Thoreau's spirituality also recalls the founder of the Quaker movement, George Fox, whom Thoreau names at least once, and who preached reliance on the "Inner Light." It also suggests an echo of New England's antinomian, or anti-law, Puritans, such as Anne Hutchinson, who put having Christ in one's heart above strict observance of the

Law of Moses—for which belief she was tried, convicted, and banished by the Puritan colony. Those who knew Thoreau or wrote about him soon after his death compared him to such reformers and ascetics. Isaac Hecker, a spiritual seeker and Transcendentalist who later became a Catholic priest and a founder of the Paulist Fathers, and who unsuccessfully badgered Thoreau to accompany him on travels around Europe, said of Thoreau, "Had he lived in the fifth century he would have been a father of the desert." Emerson, too, in a line he cut from his eulogy, called Thoreau nearest to "the old monks in their ascetic religion." And fifteen years after his death, Alexander Hay Japp, a native Scot who wrote under the pen name H. A. Page, compared Thoreau to St. Francis. "I see a kind of real likeness between this so-called 'Stoic' of America, with his unaffected love for the slave, his wonderful sympathies and attractions for the lower creatures, his simplicities, and his liking for the labors of the hand, and that St. Francis."[14]

A Protestant's Progress

Behind Thoreau's eclectic views, the church of his childhood had a profound effect on him, despite his vexed relationship with it. His mature spirituality drew in different ways on his Puritan heritage, Protestant reformational zeal, and Harvard's rational Unitarianism. It was out of dissatisfaction with the dryness of the latter that Transcendentalism emerged, initially as a religious movement and only later as a literary and social one. Like that of his Transcendentalist peers, Thoreau's spirituality was marked by practices, including journal keeping, reading, contemplation, moral introspection, and reading the natural world as a second scripture—all of which drew heavily on historic Protestant devotional disciplines. Christian poetics are plowed through his works. *Walden's* twenty-one allusions to the Gospel of Matthew give parts of it the flavor of a New England version of the Sermon on the Mount. "I think *Pilgrim's Progress* is the best sermon which has been preached on this text," Thoreau wrote of the New Testament in *A Week*. References to the "Delectable Mountains," toward which John Bunyan's pilgrim hero journeyed, appear in *A Week*, *Walden*, his *Journal*, and his letters. Thoreau's cabin, for example, was located in one of the "rare and delectable places" in the universe.[15]

Thoreau rarely identified as Protestant. One the very few times he did was when he referred in his *Journal* to Luther, the Quaker founder, and the author of *The Pilgrim's Progress*. "Do not we Protestants," he asked in 1859, "know the likeness of Luther, Fox, Bunyan, when we see it?" Yet Thoreau shows his Protestant formation in his many pointed or satirical comments about the first question in the Puritans' 1647 Westminster Shorter Catechism. In *Walden* he appears to contest the answer, declaring that most men "have *somewhat hastily* concluded that it is the chief end of man here to 'glorify God and enjoy him forever.'" Thoreau's cleverness obscures his meaning, which is not to reject such a life purpose. He objects rather that people have accepted this wisdom *too hastily*. Thoreau skewers the catechism throughout his *Journal*, for example, calling the destruction of trees in order to build a church a peculiar way of glorifying God.[16]

Loath though he was to admit, however, Thoreau was a Protestant at heart. Still, if he couldn't quite shake his Puritan heritage, neither was he bound to it. He put his own synthesis of the myriad influences on his spirituality ahead of any single one of them, and his experience ahead of any thought. Nevertheless, Thoreau was imprinted by belief in his youth— stamped by a yearning to believe. And he remained so even after he no longer held the particular beliefs with which he was raised.

Two weeks after beginning his *Journal*, Thoreau recognized that it would take a long time to sift the gold in his pan. "Truth strikes us from behind, and in the dark, as well as from before and in broad daylight," he wrote November 5, 1837, recalling Emily Dickinson's as yet unpublished injunction "Tell all the truth but tell it slant." Then, a week later, Thoreau was even more humble. "I yet lack discernment to distinguish the whole lesson of today; but it is not lost—it will come to me at last."[17]

THREE

To Reverence, Not to Fear

The basic outlines of Thoreau's iconoclastic faith can be seen in his early *Journal* and poetry, written while he was still in his twenties (roughly between 1837 and 1847). His religious thought would ebb and flow with internal tides, but its core would remain a reverence for the sacredness of life and an aspiration to embrace and be embraced by the mystery it represented. He also disclosed in his early writings the belief he developed at Harvard in the eternal now.

Thoreau expressed his religious impulse in a college essay in October 1836. The purpose of education, he wrote, should be "continuously to remind man of his mysterious relation to God and nature." Although he would conceive of that relation in different ways, he would contemplate it until his death thirty-six years later.[1]

Thoreau's early writings, especially his poems of the late 1830s and early 1840s, are suffused with a personal and even tender sense of God's presence. "I wish I could be as still as God is," he wrote in December 1841. On January 7 of the new

year, he wrote, "The great God is very calm withal. How super-
fluous is any excitement in his creatures! He listens equally
to the prayers of the believer and the unbeliever." Four days
later, on January 11, 1842, his brother, John, died—a severe
shock and indelible loss for him. If anything, however, it in-
creased Thoreau's reliance on God, at least during his darkest
grief. "What if you or I be dead?" he would write in March.
"God is alive still." *Piety* is a word that rarely escapes progres-
sive lips today, but it comes from the Latin *pius*, for dutiful,
devout, loyal, faithful, and of a pure (*purus*) heart—all qualities that describe Thoreau.[2]

Such devotional sincerity becomes sparser in his later
work, as we will see in chapter 9. He expresses his belief in
the divine in less positivistic terms, and it becomes less dependent on the category of God. "The communications from
the gods to us are still deep and sweet, indeed, but scanty and
transient," he would write in 1856, "enough only to keep alive
the memory of the past." Thoreau's elegiac laments about having become spiritually dulled and bereft must be viewed skep-
tically, however, as they often covertly call attention to the
exalted heights that his spiritual consciousness could reach.
Even after his "turn to science" in the 1850s, Thoreau periodically recorded episodes of exuberant spiritual insight and
referred to God in ways that convey an unambiguous assump-
tion of God's presence.[3]

Thoreau began his *Journal* on October 22, 1837 (apparently after Emerson asked him if he kept one), and he
did not dawdle in voicing his spiritual yearnings. The entire work, as published in fourteen volumes in 1906, would
grow to 1.85 million words, but on the inside cover of his
very first notebook, he inscribed an epitaph from the Christian metaphysical poet George Herbert urging the reader to

"salute thyself" by spending time alone and investigating one's soul.

> Dare to look in thy chest; for 'tis thy own:
> And tumble up and down what thou find'st there.[4]

Then, on October 24, in a beautiful passage at the bottom of his *Journal*'s very first page, Thoreau took the decomposition of trees as a metaphor for the "second growth" of our souls. For a 20-year-old, the spiritual gravitas is astonishing.

> Every part of nature teaches that the passing away of one life is the making room for another. The oak dies down to the ground, leaving within its rind a rich virgin mould, which will impart a vigorous life to an infant forest. The pine leaves a sandy and sterile soil, the harder woods a strong and fruitful mould. So this constant abrasion and decay makes the soil of my future growth. As I live now so shall I reap. If I grow pines and birches, my virgin mould will not sustain the oak; but pines and birches, or, perchance, weeds and brambles, will constitute my second growth.

Fear Not the Divine

Thoreau also conveyed his reverence in a Harvard assignment in March 1837. The essay was an evaluation of Edmund Burke's influential 1757 treatise, "A Philosophical Enquiry into the Origin of Our Ideas of the Sublime and Beautiful." In it, Burke argues that we encounter the sublime in overpowering displays of God's power and awful majesty. The fear and trembling we feel in response reveals the sublime. "Terror," Thoreau quoted Burke, "is in all cases whatsoever, either more openly or latently, the ruling principle of the sublime."[5]

The college senior brazenly rejected Burke's "shock and awe" view of the term. "The Deity," Thoreau wrote, "would be reverenced, not feared." And: "Whatever is grand, wonderful, or mysterious, *may* be a source of the sublime," but "terror inevitably injures, and, if excessive, may entirely destroy its effect." The sublime, he said, is a different kind of awe—one that induces reverence, humility, and respect. We come away from an experience of the sublime awed by the prospect of what lies beyond us—moved, at times, to the point of gratitude and worship. "I would make an inherent respect, or reverence, which certain objects are fitted to demand, that ruling principle." Reverence, he continued, will outlive the terror to which Burke refers "and operate to exalt and distinguish us, when fear shall be no more." Our response to the sublime and beautiful in nature was for Thoreau the very taproot of religion.

> Yes, that principle which prompts us to pay an involuntary homage to the infinite, the incomprehensible, the sublime, forms the very basis of our religion. It is a principle implanted in us by our Maker, a part of our very selves; we cannot eradicate it, we cannot resist it.[6]

To *revere* comes from the Latin *revereri*, which means to observe with respect or to fear and is based on the Indo-European root *wer*, to perceive or watch out for. To revere, for Thoreau, is to truly see something, to value it and be humbled by it—not in fear, but in awe. It was to be *drawn* to something, even to adore it. Any reverence, even for a material thing, Thoreau said, proceeds from an elevation of character. "How happens it that we reverence the stones which fall from another planet, and not the stones which belong to this?" he asked. "It would imply the regeneration of mankind, if they were to become elevated enough to truly worship sticks and stones."[7]

Discovering a patch of wildness in his domesticated landscape, Thoreau expressed "something akin to reverence" for the primitive, uncultivated land and a desire to worship it.

> I see that all is not garden and cultivated field and crops, that there are square rods in Middlesex County as purely primitive and wild as they were a thousand years ago, which have escaped the plow and the axe and the scythe and the cranberry-rake, little oases of wildness in the desert of our civilization, wild as a square rod on the moon, supposing it to be uninhabited. I believe almost in the personality of such planetary matter, feel something akin to reverence for it, can even worship it as terrene, titanic matter extant in my day. We are so different we admire each other, we healthily attract one another. I love it as a maiden.[8]

Reverence here, however, does not mean obeisance to dead religious forms. In 1837, Thoreau also read *On Religion*, by the liberal French philosopher Benjamin Constant, which argues that formal religion impedes the moral sentiment. Writing almost forty years after Schleiermacher's theological clarion call, Constant was a Romantic who also believed that interior religious experience was the basis of religion. Echoing Constant, Thoreau was soon rejecting Religion with a capital *R*. "With by far the greater part of mankind, religion is a habit, or rather, habit is religion," he wrote in another college essay. "Their views of things are illiberal and contracted. . . . However paradoxical it may seem, it appears to me that to reject Religion is the first step toward moral excellence."[9]

A Great Cave

Thoreau's sense of reverence was borne out dramatically in the most unlikely of places: a Catholic cathedral. In 1850 he visited Montreal's Notre-Dame Basilica. He initially experienced some bafflement, as he wrote in his essay "A Yankee in Canada." Unimpressed by Catholicism, Thoreau sarcastically allowed that it might be admirable "if the priest were quite omitted" and suggested that, if he could, he might visit such a church himself "some Monday." But doing so would be unneeded in Concord, where "our forests are such a church, far grander and more sacred."[10]

Nevertheless, to his surprise, something about the silence and solemnity of this "great cave in the midst of a city" struck him. He was touched "by the quiet religious atmosphere of the place," and by the end of his visit he saw something missing in Yankee culture.

> I soon found my way to the church of Notre Dame. . . . The Catholic are the only churches which I have seen worth remembering, which are not almost wholly profane. I do not speak only of the rich and splendid like this, but of the humblest of them as well. Coming from the hurrahing mob and the rattling carriages, we pushed aside the listed door of this church, and found ourselves instantly in an atmosphere which might be sacred to thought and religion, if one had any.

Two women who had "stolen a moment from the concerns of the day" sat alone. But even if there had been fifty people, the place would have just as solitary. Presently, a "troop" of young Canadians in homespun clothing came in and kneeled somewhat awkwardly in the aisle, in front of the altar, before their devotions.

> As if you were to catch some farmer's sons from Marlboro, come to cattle-show, silently kneeling in Concord meeting-house some Wednesday! Would there not soon be a mob peeping in at the windows? It is true, these Roman Catholics, priests and all, impress me as a people who have fallen far behind the significance of their symbols. It is as if an ox had strayed into a church and were trying to bethink himself. Nevertheless, they are capable of reverence; but we Yankees are a people in whom this sentiment has nearly died out, and in this respect we cannot bethink ourselves even as oxen.

An Eternal Natal Hour

Thoreau's reverence and spiritual aspirations are even more pronounced in his youthful poems, especially "Inspiration," which he wrote around 1841 and later wove into *A Week*. It opens with a declaration of surrender to the infinite: "Whatever we leave to God, God does / And blesses us." The poet says that if he takes pride in his literary genius, nothing will come of his verse, but if "with bended neck" he bows to the flame in his soul, it will endure. Such humility turns his senses into portals to the divine; the poet, once merely "sensual," becomes "sensible," or alert, in mind as well as body—a play on the meaning of *sense* that Thoreau will invoke many times. Now the poet hears beyond the range of sound and sees beyond the verge of sight.[11]

> I hearing get, who had but ears,
> And sight, who had but eyes before,

I moments live, who lived but years,
And truth discern, who knew but learning's lore.

I hear beyond the range of sound,
I see beyond the range of sight,
New earths and skies and seas around,
And in my day the sun doth pale his light.

The poem then shifts to another strand in Thoreau's religious thought. The awakened poet enters a moment that fuses past, present, and future. "Now chiefly is my natal hour / And only now my prime of life." Thoreau's spirituality was centered around time as well as place. He revered not only the sacred space of Walden Pond or a nameless swamp, but also sacred time, his "natal hour." For Thoreau, the present moment, when experienced fully, is the meeting of two eternities, the past and the future. "I have just heard the flicker among the oaks on the hillside ushering in a new dynasty," he wrote Sunday, April 3, 1842. "It is the age and youth of time. . . . The summer's eternity is reestablished by this note. All sights and sounds are heard both in time and eternity. And when the eternity of any sight or sound strikes the eye or ear—they are intoxicated with delight."

Thoreau's immersion in the classics at Harvard deepened his belief that we live in the same original moment as those who walked in primordial dawn of poetry and myth. It was a realm of time not counted on the town clock, an endless moment of fable and possibility—an island in time that Christian mystics have called the eternal now, a term that Emerson also used. "In the presence of nature," he wrote in his 1837–38 lecture series on "Human Culture," "a man of feeling is not suffered to lose sight of the instant of creation. The world was not made a long time ago. Nature is an Eternal Now."[12]

The idea of the eternal now has a long philosophical heritage that can be traced back at least to Augustine, who argued in his *Confessions* that "neither future nor past exists, and it is inexact language to speak of three times—past, present, and future." The twentieth-century philosopher and process theologian Alfred North Whitehead saw it as the basis of the religious sentiment. "The foundation of reverence," he wrote, "is this perception, that the present holds within itself the complete sum of existence, backwards and forwards, that whole amplitude of time, which is eternity."[13]

Thoreau would seem to agree. In *A Week* he tells us that "one veil hangs over past, present, and future." In 1842, he wondered why old things, like rusty nails, betray their age by their appearance. "Why," he asked, "does God not make some mistake to show us time is a delusion?" He also asked that year, "What, then can I do to hasten that other time, or that space where there shall be not time," when "there will be no discords in my life?"[14]

One of my favorite passages in Thoreau's *Journal* is about cracking the nut of time. As he stood along the Mill Brook in Concord one October, a profusion of red oak acorns fell like hail, sounding like muskrats plunging as they hit the water. Although Thoreau couldn't eat the acorns raw, he vowed to feed his soul on their remembered beauty. He dreamed of a winter evening when these "untasted" "nuts of the gods" would finally be cracked in his memory and their flavors released—at which moment time would suddenly be no more.

> How munificent is Nature to create this profusion of wild fruit, as it were merely to gratify our eyes! Though inedible they are more wholesome to my immortal part, and stand by me longer, than the fruits which I eat. If they had been plums or chestnuts I should have eaten them on the spot

and probably forgotten them. They would have afforded only a momentary gratification, but being acorns, I remember, and as it were feed on, them still. They are untasted fruits forever in store for me. I know not of their flavor as yet. That is postponed to some still unimagined winter evening. These which we admire but do not eat are nuts of the gods. When time is no more we shall crack them.[15]

Spiritual Aspirant

Walking in the woods in 1841, Thoreau bent down a bough in his path. "I bend the twig and write my prayers on it; then letting it go, the bough springs up and shows the scrawl to heaven. As if it were not kept shut in my desk, but were as public a leaf as any in nature." It was a characteristic gesture for him. Thoreau's essential religious stance is that of a postulant, a supplicant, an aspirant. At different times he called himself an "anchorite" (an old term for a religious recluse) and a "yogin." For all his petulance and arrogance, aspiration to a higher stage of spiritual development was at core of his being. "It is with infinite yearning and aspiration that I seek solitude." There is but one obligation, Thoreau also said, and that is to obey the highest dictates of one's conscience. "Did you ever hear of a man who had striven all his life faithfully and singly toward an object and in no measure obtained it?" he asked in a letter to Blake. "If a man constantly aspires, is he not elevated?"[16]

Oliver Cromwell is reputed to have written in his pocket Bible, "Qui cessat esse melior cessat esse bonus" (He who ceases to be better, ceases to be good). Aspiration was not about being better for Thoreau. It was about being. "My desire for knowledge is intermittent," he wrote in 1851, "but my desire to commune with the spirit of the universe, to be intoxicated even with the fumes, call it, of that divine nectar, to bear my head through atmospheres and over heights unknown to my feet, is perennial and constant."[17]

Thoreau reverenced the divinity within him as well as without, in accord with the Transcendentalist belief in self-culture, or the cultivation of the soul. Trust in God was actually to rely on oneself, he wrote on January 29, 1841. "God is not our ally when we shrink," only when we are bold. "If by trusting in God, you lose any particle of your vigor, trust in him no longer. When you trust, do not lay aside your armor but put it on, and buckle it tighter." He enthused in his *Journal* about the possibility of personal spiritual growth. "That I love and reverence my life!" he wrote on July 16, 1851. "That I am better fitted for a lofty society today than I was yesterday!"

Four years later he was discouraged, but he held to the same hope: "Pursue some path, however narrow and crooked, in which you can walk with love and reverence."[18]

FOUR

The Seen and the Unseen

In addition to his fundamental reverence, other elements of Thoreau's religious thought that were evident by the mid-1840s were his understanding of religion as a way of living, his practice of attention as a spiritual discipline, his sense of wonder, and his consciousness of an unseen order.

Religion for Thoreau was not a compilation of beliefs but a set of internal possibilities and choices about how to live, what to notice, what to love. "The only prayer for a brave man is to be a doing"—to be putting belief into practice, he wrote in 1840. "This is the prayer that is heard." Thoreau said he was more interested in the attitudes and lives of history's great spiritual teachers than in their teachings. As a philosophical idealist, he revered Plato, of course, but he also wanted to know how Plato made a living. It makes a difference if he lived by the dictates of his philosophy, Thoreau said, or if he found it "easier to live because his aunt remembered him in her will." Thoreau's pragmatic view of philosophy is supported by ancient religious wisdom. "Truth is high," said Guru

Nanak, the early sixteenth-century founder of Sikhism, "but higher still is truthful living."[1]

So, too, with religion. Thoreau's creed was in how he lived. "For my part if I have any creed it is so to live as to preserve and increase the susceptibleness of my nature to noble impulses," he wrote his friend Isaiah Thornton Williams. "First to observe if any light shine of me and then faithfully to follow it."[2]

That is why Thoreau's antislavery and social justice writings, including "Civil Disobedience" and his later defense of John Brown, appeal to biblical justice and to God as a source of higher law. Although Thoreau faulted the Hebrew Bible for being coarser and more worldly than the Hindu scriptures, he embodied its prophetic voice and ethos in his social criticism. In his essay "Slavery in Massachusetts," Thoreau excoriated those who justified the Fugitive Slave Act of 1850 on narrow constitutional grounds, calling them "the servants of man, and the worst of men, rather than the servants of God."

> The question is not whether you or your grandfather, seventy years ago, entered into an agreement to serve the devil, and that service is not accordingly now due; but whether you will not now, for once and at last, serve God, in spite of your own past recreancy or that of your ancestors, and obey that eternal and only just CONSTITUTION which He, and not any Jefferson or Adams, has written in your being.[3]

Thoreau was puzzled when a farmer who visited him at Walden told him that he had not had a bath in fifteen years. Thoreau regarded bathing in Concord's rivers and ponds as essential to renew his spirit as well as his body. "Now what kind of religion could his be?" he wondered about the farmer. Thoreau had a similar reaction one Sunday evening when he spotted the town barber alone in boat on the river headed to remote Fair Haven Bay. "He is quite alone, thus far from town, and so quiet and sensibly employed . . . that I think of him as having experienced religion."[4]

However, religion was not *only* a matter of outward acts. It had to spring from a fundamental way of being, a perception of the divinity within oneself and of the sacrality of all life. Thus each morning at Walden Thoreau not only swam in the pond but bathed his intellect in another sacred body—the Bhagavad Gita.

A Habit of Attention

Thoreau's habit of attention was simultaneously the basis of his work as a naturalist and his primary spiritual discipline. Attention thickened his experience of the natural world and drew him into deeper contact with ultimate reality. It made his nature studies acts of contemplation. "The eye has many qualities which belong more to God than to man," he wrote in 1841. To attend to something is to be *inclined* to see it, to notice it. It is also to penetrate the surface of things and, for Thoreau, to detect the divine presence. The farmer may cut or trample over plants every day in his work, Thoreau said, but if he "favorably attends" to them, he may be overcome by their beauty. Not that this is easy. "Each natural object" is "content to be part of the mystery which is God." Thoreau admired the works of the Hudson River school painter Thomas Cole and would have agreed with him that we must "learn the laws by which the Eternal doth sublime and sanctify his works, that we may see the hidden glory veiled from vulgar eyes."[5]

That is why attention requires intention—an expectation and desire to distinguish *what is* from *what appears* and to see the holy hidden in the ordinary. In "Autumnal Tints," Thoreau's awareness of an immortality in nature rests on a willed attention to the life force in the litter of fallen leaves. While Thoreau believed we must look in order to see, he also worried, conversely, that observing too narrowly or too hard can constrain true seeing. The eye must also saunter. "Be not preoccupied with looking. Go not to the object; let it come to you." To pay attention is not to examine as with a microscope but to behold.[6]

In essence, to be attentive was to be awake for Thoreau. "To be awake is to be alive," he wrote in *Walden*. "I have never yet met a man who was quite awake. How could I have looked him in the face?" Descending into a dark cellar to fetch an armload of wood, he heard what at first sounded like a routine noise, "but when, as it were by accident, I reverently attended to the hint, I found that it was the voice of a God who had followed me down cellar to speak to me. How many communications may we not lose through inattention?"[7]

The naturalist and critic Loren Eiseley wrote fifty years ago that "God asks nothing of the highest soul but attention." Another twentieth-century figure, the French philosopher and mystic Simone Weil, wrote, "Attention taken to the highest degree, is the same thing as prayer. It presupposes faith and love." Thoreau, I think, would have understood them both. *Walden*, his most religious work, is a prose poem against distraction. He believed that capitalism, with its machines, markets, mindless work, and trivial entertainment, was damaging people's capacity for reverence. "I believe that the mind can be permanently profaned by the habit of attending to trivial things, so that all our thoughts shall be tinged with triviality," he wrote in his essay "Life without Principle," which grew out of his experience at Walden. (*Trivial*, a word Thoreau used often, derives from the Latin *trivium*, for the meeting place of three roads. Thoreau showed his knowledge of this when he described trivialness as "a place where three highways of sin meet.")[8]

Attention for Thoreau, or "the discipline of looking always at what is to be seen," as he describes it in *Walden*, is a sacred duty.

> I often perceive how near I had come to admitting into my mind the details of some trivial affair—the news of the street; and I am astonished to observe how willing men are to lumber their minds with such rubbish—to permit idle rumors and incidents of the most insignificant kind to intrude on ground which should be sacred to thought. Shall the mind be a public arena, where the affairs of the street and the gossip of the tea-table chiefly are discussed? Or shall it be a quarter of heaven itself, an hypaethral [open air] temple, consecrated to the service of the gods?[9]

Channels of Wonder

Wonder at the natural world was the wellspring of Thoreau's spirituality. His daily visits to the woods, fields, and waters of Concord set his spiritual wheels in motion. The crowing of a cock at dawn, light slanting in golden streams through the aisles of the forest at sunset, the cheep of a sparrow, the aromatic smell of pine, or a delicate robin nest could elicit his awe. "All the phenomena of nature need to be seen from the point of view of wonder and awe," he wrote. Even lightning "needs to be regarded with the same serenity as the most familiar and innocent phenomena."[10]

Thoreau's soul expanded out of doors. The woods contain an "inexpressible happiness." "All their sounds and sights are elixirs to my spirit" he wrote in 1841. "They possess a divine health. God is not more well. Every sound is inspiriting and fraught with the same mysterious assurance, from the creaking of the boughs in January to the soft sough of the wind in July."[11]

Thoreau's senses were the channels of that wonder. "Thou openest all my senses," he also wrote in 1841. His acute sensory portals delivered such rapturous moments of oneness with the universe that we must take Thoreau seriously when he calls himself a mystic. "Depend upon it that, rude and careless as I am, I would fain practice the yoga faithfully," he wrote Blake in 1849. "To some extent, and at rare intervals, even I am a yogin."[12]

Sounds penetrated to a deeper silence within, as if they were "the interjections of God." Thoreau's ear seemed to bypass his logical faculties and communicate directly with his soul. "The profane never hear music," he wrote in 1840. "The holy ever hear it. It is God's voice, the divine breath audible. Where it is heard, there is a Sabbath." Certain sounds could lift him to the point of ecstasy.[13]

> There are a few sounds still which never fail to affect me. . . . The strains of the Aeolian harp and of the wood thrush are the truest and loftiest preachers that I know now left on this earth. I know of no missionaries to us heathen comparable to them. They, as it were, lift us up in spite of ourselves. They intoxicate, they charm us. . . . I would be drunk, drunk, drunk, dead drunk to this world with it forever. He that hath ears, let him hear. The contact of sound with a human ear whose hearing is pure and unimpaired is coincident with an ecstasy.[14]

That wonder diminished over time, but Thoreau never lost it. At the sound of the wind in trees, "I recover my spirits, my spirituality, through my hearing," he wrote in 1851. The next year he asked, referring to the eerie sounds emitted by Concord's telegraph poles, "Why was it made that man should be thrilled to his inmost being by the vibrating of a wire?" Some of the most exuberant passages in Thoreau's *Journal* record moments when he was lifted out of a desultory mood by a sensory experience as ordinary as the chant of crickets, the lowing of cattle, or the colors of the autumn woods.[15]

A visit to Fair Haven Cliffs before dawn on June 17, 1852, ferried him back to the primordial dawn of religion. "I love that early twilight hour when the crickets still creak right on with such dewy faith and promise, as if it were still night, expressing the innocence of morning, when the creak of the cricket is fresh and bedewed. It buries Greece and Rome past resurrection. The earth song of the cricket! Before Christianity was, it is. Health! health! health! is the burden of its song."

The following June, Thoreau was enchanted by what he called "the gospel of the wood thrush," a bird whose note affected "the flow and tenor of my thought, my fancy and imagination."[16]

It lifts and exhilarates me. It is inspiring. It is a medicative draught to my soul. It is an elixir to my eyes and a fountain of youth to all my senses. It changes all hours to an eternal morning. It banishes all trivialness. It reinstates me in my dominion, makes me the lord of creation, is chief musician of my court. This minstrel sings in a time, a heroic age, with which no event in the village can be contemporary. . . . I long for wildness, a nature which I cannot put my foot through, woods where the wood thrush forever sings, where the hours are early morning ones, and there is dew on the grass, and the day is forever unproved, where I might have a fertile unknown for a soil about me.[17]

An Unseen Order

The very earthiness of Thoreau's experience points to a central paradox in his religion, between his attachment to and love of the "solid and sunny earth" and his sense of something beyond the physical world. The earth is the "basis" of all religion, Thoreau declares, yet he also had an indefinable, indefatigable yearning for something "beyond the range of sound and beyond the verge of sight," as he wrote in *A Week*. In spiritually elevated states, this sometimes led him to a sense of not being entirely at home in the world.[18]

James recognized what he called "the reality of the unseen" as a core feature of religion, an idea that can be traced at least to the apostle Paul, who spoke of faith in things unseen. All our attitudes, whether conscious or not, James wrote in *Varieties*, are due to the "objects" of our minds—things to which we respond *as if* they do exist, although they may not be present to our senses. "In the broadest and most general terms possible," he wrote, "the life of religion, consists of the belief that there is an unseen order, and that our supreme good lies in harmoniously adjusting ourselves thereto. This belief and this adjustment are the religious attitude in the soul." One could describe Thoreau's life as an effort to "harmoniously adjust" himself to the natural world and the mystery it contains.[19]

Thoreau's spirituality straddled both sides of this paradox—his desire to find the hard bottom to life and his attraction to the unseen layers above, below, and within it. In January 1842, for example, he was physically and emotionally invigorated by a thawing south wind that melted the snow, revealing the naked ground.

In such a season a perfume seems to exhale from the earth itself and the south wind melts my integuments also. Then is she my mother earth. I derive a real vigor from the scent of the gale wafted over the naked ground, as from strong meats, and realize again how man is the pensioner of Nature. We are always conciliated and cheered when we are fed by [such] an influence, and our needs are felt to be part of the domestic economy of Nature.[20]

Yet a month later, Thoreau reflected that the best part of nature is *never actually felt*. Indeed it retreats at his approach. He seemed to accept that "this faith and expectation" that he carried into nature would never be tangible to his senses. "I was always conscious of sounds in nature which my ears could never hear—that I caught but the prelude to a strain. She always retreats as I advance. Away behind and behind is she and her meaning. Will not this faith and expectation make itself to ears at length? I never saw to the end, nor heard to the end; but the best part was unseen and unheard."[21]

In Thoreau's theological universe, he called what we think of as the spiritual or the ideal as "the real," while he often called the world of empirical reality "the actual." Thus "when we are awake to the real world, we are asleep to the actual," he wrote in 1841. "The sinful drowse to eternity, and the virtuous to time"—the sinful are oblivious to eternity, while the virtuous are oblivious to the profane time of the railroad schedule. The catch, Thoreau observed many times, is that there is no train, no way "in," to the spiritual—at least, no way to travel there bodily.[22]

"Though I am old enough to have discovered that the dreams of youth are not to be realized in this state of existence," Thoreau wrote at age 26, "yet I think it would be the next greatest happiness always to be allowed to look under the eyelids of time and contemplate the perfect steadily with the clear understanding that I do not attain to it."[23]

In his episodes of spiritual exaltation, Thoreau saw himself as somehow "shipwrecked" on Earth, as he put it, unable to penetrate down, or up, to the highest, or deepest, level of reality—the level of the unheard and unseen. Three times in his *Journal*, Thoreau compared his fate to the plight of Moses, who never actually reached the Promised Land, toward which he had journeyed for forty years. Thoreau understood that poignant gap between yearning and fulfillment. "We daily live the fate of Moses, who only looked into the Promised land from [Mount] Pisgah before he died."[24]

It seems that Thoreau could choose whether to see the physical, or the "actual," and the spiritual, or the "real," depending on his mood or his purpose. He had a unique ability to see nature as fact with one eye, as he did during his exacting study of natural phenomena, and as parable with the other. On a moonlight walk, with the earth bathed in a dim religious light, Thoreau could turn the most prosaic precincts into paradisial pastures.

> On one side of man is the actual, and on the other the ideal. The former is the province of the reason. But it cannot reach forward into the ideal without blindness. The moon was made to rule by night, but the sun to rule by day. Reason will be but a pale cloud, like the moon, when one ray of divine light comes to illumine the soul.[25]

Touched by a Battery

Thoreau's Transcendentalism allowed him to make the shift from one way of seeing to another. It was a matter of how he paid attention. There is perhaps no more beautiful or palpable example of his shifting from the "actual" to the "real" than in his description of lesser redpolls, a species of small bird, feeding on birch seeds on the snow in 1855.[26]

After the first snow that November, Thoreau came upon "a flock of delicate crimson-tinged birds" cheerfully twittering and shaking down the seeds on the sunny side the wood "as if it were high midsummer to them." The delicacy of form and ripeness of color of these tropical-looking creatures in so barren a season transfixed him. "Their maker gave them the last touch and launched them forth the day of the Great Snow. He made this bitter imprisoning cold before which man quails— but he made at the same time these warm and glowing creatures to twitter and be at home in it."

All the fountains of nature might have been sealed up, but at the edge of a birch wood, a flock of these "birds of paradise" was feeding on the seeds as if they were "a flower created to be now in bloom, a peach to be now first fully ripe on its stem." The sight was so compelling that it almost gave Thoreau a kind of charge, as if he had touched a battery.

> I had a vision of these birds as I stood in the swamps. I saw this familiar—too familiar—fact at a different angle, and I was charmed and haunted by it. It is only necessary to behold thus the least fact or phenomenon, however familiar, from a point a hair's breadth aside from our habitual path or routine, to be overcome, enchanted by its beauty and significance.
>
> My body is all sentient. As I go here or there, I am tickled by this or that I come in contact with, as if I touched the wires of a battery. . . . The age of miracles is each moment thus returned. Now it is wild apples, now river reflections, now a flock of lesser redpolls.
>
> We get only transient and partial glimpses of the beauty

of the world. Standing at the right angle, we are dazzled by
the colors of the rainbow in colorless ice. . . . I am surprised
and enchanted often by some quality which I cannot detect.
I have seen an attribute of another world and condition of
things. It is a wonderful fact that I should be affected—that
this fruit should be borne in me, sprung from a seed finer
than the spores of fungi, floated from other atmospheres!
Finer than the dust caught in the sails of vessels a thousand
miles from land! Here the invisible seeds settle, and spring,
and bear flowers and fruits of immortal beauty.

Thoreau plugged into a spiritual current in such moments
and saw with new eyes. Even transient and partial glimpses of
beauty were enough for him to be enchanted by some quality
he could not quite detect. His wonder at the sight of the lesser
redpolls feeding on birch seeds on the snow is of a piece with
his vision of immortal beauty borne of invisible seeds, uniting
his capacity to see what was before him with his intuition of
the unseen.

FIVE

A Puritan Golden Calf

Thoreau's reputation as an apostate is partly deserved. The chief reason is the ferocity of his attack on historical Christianity in *A Week on the Concord and Merrimack Rivers*. Thoreau would excoriate the clergy and formal religion for the rest of his life—notably, in his sardonic take on evangelical camp meetings in *Cape Cod*. But it is his first book, published in 1849, that gave him his pitchfork and horns in the popular imagination. You know you've crossed a line when both your literary patron and your own aunt accuse you of impious sacrilege, which is what happened when Horace Greeley and Thoreau's Aunt Maria read *A Week*. Like much of Thoreau's writing before he achieved his perfectly modulated, chiseled-in-stone prose style in *Walden*, the book *A Week* is both brilliant and overweening at once.

Thoreau's Harvard classmate John Weiss, the son of a Jewish barber in Worcester, who later became a Unitarian minister, was one of the few people then who seems to have understood what Thoreau was doing. "It is in the interest of holiness

that he speaks slightingly of Scripture and its holy men," he
wrote in the *Christian Examiner* in 1865.[1]

Thoreau wrote *A Week* before he was 30. It is ostensibly the
narrative of a two-week boat trip from Concord, Massachusetts, to the White Mountains, which he took in 1839 with his
brother, John, but it is more of an extended (and digressive)
meditation on nature's truths and the triumph of the eternal
over the transient. The trip is compressed into seven days,
with each of its seven chapters representing a day of the week.
Given that the Bible begins with the first seven days of creation, the scholar Linck Johnson has called it Thoreau's private Book of Genesis. Thoreau had begun drafting parts of *A
Week* into his *Journal* before he moved to Walden Pond in July
1845, and by the time he left, in September 1847, it was largely
finished. One of his purposes in writing it was to remove religion from its nineteenth-century institutional context and
reframe it in ancient ones—Eastern as well as Western.[2]

Thoreau's animus against the church in *A Week* was not
entirely religious. He distrusted institutions of all kinds—
schools, government, and philanthropic societies as well as
religious bodies. He was also philosophically opposed to the
kind of abstract, labyrinthine systems of thought that Christianity that has historically generated. The moral cowardice
that ministers in his day displayed with their halting, half-
hearted support of the antislavery movement also appalled
him. (Concord's churches gradually fell in line with abolition,
but only after initial resistance.) Religion without the moral
law was no religion at all for Thoreau. The clergy were not at
liberty to follow their moral conscience, he thought, because
the church had sold its soul to power, prestige, and property.

> The church! It is eminently the timid institution, and the
> heads and pillars of it are constitutionally and by principle

the greatest cowards in the community. The voice that goes up from [the church] is not so brave and so cheering as that which rises from the frog-ponds of the land. . . . There is nothing to redeem the bigotry and moral cowardice of New-Englanders in my eyes.[3]

Thoreau, of course, did have objections to the church of his day on religious grounds, and I would like to consider three. First, that Christianity's exclusivist claims to truth fostered sectarianism and bigotry. Second, that its doctrines and creeds were a misguided effort to freeze-dry the divine in words. Third, that the meetinghouse worshipped a revelation in the past, not the one present in each moment.[4]

Pagoda Worship

A Week was an assault not on the Christian ideal but on what Thoreau called the "respectable" Christianity of his day, which he saw as a kind of Puritan golden calf—an idolatrous substitute for the real thing. Indeed, Thoreau used Christian theological values and scripture to tweak his neighbors for their "barren want of faith." The church was dead to Thoreau because it was disconnected from nature. "A temple was anciently 'an open place without a roof,'" he wrote his friend Harry Blake three years after *A Week* came out, "whose walls served merely to shut out the world and direct the mind toward heaven; but a modern meeting-house shuts out the heavens." It may appear that Thoreau is replacing religion with nature in *A Week*. In fact, he is trying to make religion more authentic by integrating it with nature. A person "needs not only to be spiritualized, but *naturalized*, on the soil of earth," he wrote in the conclusion.[5]

To Thoreau, the "respectable" church was so smugly moralistic and complicit in the exploitation of both human beings and the natural world as to represent the *opposite* of religion. It blessed the "commercial spirit" of the day, a materialistic ethos he denounced in a speech at his commencement in 1837. "There is no infidelity, now-a-days, so great as that which prays, and keeps the sabbath, and rebuilds the churches," Thoreau wrote in *A Week*. "The sealer of the South Pacific preaches a truer doctrine. One is sick at heart of this pagoda worship."[6]

In pressing each of his objections, however, Thoreau disclosed the depth of his religious instincts. He often did so, however, by means of subtle rhetorical shifts and caveats that are easily lost amid his invective. He sounds like a heretic as he detonates historical Christianity, but beneath the verbal fireworks is an openness to God and to the world as a divine creation. "The god that is commonly worshipped in civilized countries is not at all divine, though he bears a divine name, but is the overwhelming authority and respectability of mankind combined," Thoreau wrote. But he added, "Men reverence one another, not yet God." There is a similar twist in his dismissal of those who cling to static notions of God. "They think they love God! It is only his old clothes, of which they make scarecrows for the children," Thoreau thundered in his *Journal*, but then added, "Where will they come nearer to God than in those very children?"[7]

God Takes No Sides

Religious sectarianism flourished in America in the early decades of the nineteenth century and took off in Massachusetts after 1834, when the Puritan-descended churches yielded their established position. By 1840, the old-time Puritan churches (some of which, mostly in eastern Massachusetts, had by then turned Unitarian) were competing on Sunday with Trinitarian, Episcopalian, Methodist, Catholic, Universalist, Baptist, Quaker, Shaker, and Adventist congregations. Some five million tracts were produced devoted to William Miller's prediction of the end of the world and second coming of Christ on Tuesday, October 22, 1844, which proved to be a darker day for Miller's followers than in the way they had imagined.[8]

Thoreau would have none of it. "There are various, nay, incredible faiths; why should we be alarmed at any of them?" he wrote in the "Sunday" chapter of *A Week*. Thoreau's access to early translations of Hindu and Chinese texts, which he read in Emerson's library from 1841 to 1843, led him to imagine an amalgam of all the world's holy books as a tower of wisdom. Each of the world's scriptures spoke in some fashion to the same spiritual truths Thoreau had discovered for himself— that all forms of life are unified by a divine energy unbounded by space and time. Thoreau saw them, collectively, as a single vision expressed according to the culture of a particular place and time.[9]

His reading convinced him that pluralism was the right road to religious truth, a position he never yielded. "The Gods are of no sect; they side with no man," he wrote in 1841. Eleven years later, in 1852: "The entertaining of a single thought of a certain elevation makes all men of one religion. It is always some base alloy that creates the distinction of sects." He also indignantly slammed the racial and cultural bias and bigotry skulking behind sectarianism and Christian intolerance of other religions. "I perceive no triumphant superiority in the so-called Christian," he wrote. "As if a Christian's dog were something better than a Mahometan's!"[10]

Motions of the Soul

Another target of *A Week* are doctrines and the creeds that express them. To Thoreau, faith is fluid and contingent on experience, not settled into fixed formulations. It is less a conviction of the mind than a motion of the soul. I think Thoreau would have agreed with the late novelist and essayist Frederick Buechner, who said faith is "less a position on than a movement toward, less a sure thing than a hunch." Most people, Thoreau writes in *A Week*, accept "Father, Son, and Holy Ghost, and the like" as a truth as everlasting as the hills, "but in all my wanderings I never came across the least vestige of authority for these things."[11]

People show their faith, or lack of it, in how they live—that was Thoreau's creed. "The only faith that men recognize is a creed. But the true creed which we unconsciously live by, and which rather adopts us than we it, is quite different from the written or preached one." What mattered to Thoreau was believing, not the belief. "That we have but little faith is not sad, but that we have but little faithfulness," he wrote Blake in 1848. "By faithfulness faith is earned."[12]

The American Christian missionary movement, which began during the 1820s, fretted over "heathens," but the only heathens who bothered Thoreau were the ones who worshipped no god at all. "None of the heathen are too heathenish for me but those who hold no intercourse with their god. I love the vigorous faith of those heathen who sternly believed *something*. I say to these modern believers, don't interrupt those men's prayers."[13]

Doctrines also posed an epistemological problem. Thoreau doubted that the highest truths could be captured in rational discourse. It took not knowledge but a kind of malleable or receptive ignorance to gain some glimmer of them. Emerson also wrote, in an 1834 letter to his brother Edward, that the soul "never reasons, never proves, it simply perceives." This was an article of faith for Thoreau, who reworked that thought in his *Journal* in 1840: "The soul does not inspect but behold." To behold is to contemplate and receive with wonder.[14]

To frame God in objective terms is to put our knowledge above God's transcendence. A God whose veil can be ripped aside by the human mind is not a God worthy of being reverenced. "The destiny of the soul can never be studied by the reason, for its modes are not ecstatic," Thoreau wrote. "In the wisest calculation or demonstration I but play a game with myself . . . I cannot convince myself. God must convince."[15]

Thoreau was drawn to the Vedic texts of India in part by their openness to change and admission of uncertainty, suggesting the very opposite of doctrine. The ancient scriptures frankly acknowledged the ineffability of the divine, he noted in *A Week*.

In the very indistinctness of their theogony [the origin and descent of the gods] a sublime truth is implied. It hardly allows the reader to rest in any supreme first cause, but directly it hints at a supremer still which created the last, and the Creator is still behind increate.[16]

Doctrines harden over time into fixed lenses, or "schemes," that prevent us from seeing clearly, Thoreau believed. Instead of expressing truth, they become obstacles to it. "The wisest man preaches no doctrines," he wrote in *A Week*. "He has no scheme; he sees no rafter, not even a cobweb, against the heavens. It is clear sky. If I ever see more clearly at one time than at another, the medium through which I see is clearer. . . . Your scheme must be the framework of the universe; all other schemes will soon be ruins."[17]

God in a Frosted Bush

A third objection is that the meetinghouse worshipped an antique revelation. Most people, Thoreau thought, adhere like oysters to received wisdom. The meetinghouse reveres ancient revelations, "but any direct revelation, any original thoughts, it hates like virtue." Here, again, Emerson's influence on Thoreau was inescapable. "Our age is retrospective," begins Emerson's *Nature*, which was published during Thoreau's junior year at Harvard. "It builds the sepulchers of the fathers. . . . Why should we not enjoy an original relation to the universe? Why should we not have a poetry and philosophy of insight and not of tradition, and a religion by revelation to us, and not the history of theirs?" Religion was also here and now for Thoreau, who did not so much intentionally copy Emerson, as he was accused of doing, as to live and think in an intellectual culture that Emerson helped create. In the 1830s and '40s, as Harold Bloom has written, Emerson was "the inescapable precursor, the literary hero, the mind of the United States of America."[18]

Out in the winter woods on a Sunday in January 1853, Thoreau heard the bells of First Parish. "How much more religion in their sound, than they ever call men together to. Men obey their call and go to the stove-warmed church, though God exhibits himself to the walker in a frosted bush today, as much as in a burning one to Moses of old."[19]

The sacred was ultimate reality for Thoreau. In that sense it was *super* or intensely natural, not supernatural. He had no interest in the Spiritualism movement, spirit rapping, or the other forms of occult religion popular in the mid-nineteenth century that presumed supernatural forces and occurrences. In this he was aligned with his fellow Transcendentalists, who tended to view Spiritualism with a skepticism bordering on contempt. Emerson called it the "rathole revelation" and claimed that the adepts of Spiritualism had "mistaken flatulence for inspiration."[20]

"Concord is just as idiotic as ever in relation to the spirits and their knockings," Thoreau wrote his sister Sophia in 1852. "Most people here believe in a spiritual world which no respectable junk bottle, which had not met with a slip, would condescend to contain even a portion of for a moment—whose atmosphere would extinguish a candle let down into it, like a well that wants airing. . . . The hooting of owls, the croaking of frogs, is celestial wisdom in comparison."[21]

If he actually believed in the occult, Thoreau quipped, "I should make haste to get rid of my certificate of stock in this and the next world's enterprises, and buy a share in the first Immediate Annihilation Company. . . . Consider the dawn and the sunrise—the rainbow and the evening—the words of Christ and the aspiration of all the saints! Hear music! See, smell, taste, feel, hear—anything—and then hear these idiots, inspired by the cracking of a restless board, humbly asking, 'Please, Spirit, if you cannot answer by knocks, answer by tips of the table!!'"[22]

What he called the "real" was so sacred to Thoreau that he capitalized it in *A Week*, writing of "those faint revelations of the Real which are vouchsafed to men from time to time, or rather from eternity to eternity." God is absolute reality, the source and fullest expression of natural law. Thoreau would link revelation and reality in a famous passage in *Walden*.[23]

> Men esteem truth remote, in the outskirts of the system, behind the farthest star, before Adam and after the last man. In eternity there is indeed something true and sublime. But all these times and places and occasions are now and here. God himself culminates in the present moment, and will

never be more divine in the lapse of all the ages. And we are
enabled to apprehend at all what is sublime and noble only
by the perpetual instilling and drenching of the reality that
surrounds us.[24]

The religious ideas Thoreau developed in *A Week* have a
cheeky confidence about them, suggesting that they were ve-
hicles of his youth, but he remained faithful to the core ones
later in his life. He expressed his belief in revelation here and
now in December 1859 after John Brown's attack on slavery at
Harpers Ferry. "Commonly men live according to a formula,"
he wrote. "They remember the old formula; they do not hear
the new revelation." But people who were stirred by Brown's
actions were capable of perceiving the moral law anew.
"They, whether in the church or out of it, who adhere to the
spirit and abandon the letter, and who are accordingly called
infidel, have been foremost in this movement."[25]

Thoreau valued scripture and tradition, but only as the
beginning of the quest for spiritual truth, a principle he applied to the quest for moral truth or justice in politics and
public life. In "Civil Disobedience," he underscored the im-
portance of seeking a higher truth than the dubious legal
sanction of slavery by the US Constitution. The constitutional
view is a mere tradition without "the vitality and force of a
single living man." We must drink from the very fountains
from which truth springs, however high up the mountainside
they may be.[26]

They who know of no purer sources of truth, who have
traced up its stream no higher, stand, and wisely stand, by
the Bible and the Constitution, and drink at it there with
reverence and humanity, but they who behold where it
comes trickling into this lake or that pool, gird up their

loins once more, and continue their pilgrimage toward its fountainhead.[27]

In *A Week*, Thoreau concluded that the Christian scheme of the universe is "an ancient and tottering frame with all its boards blown off." Years later he would say even the word *church* is "spurious and artificial," and that trying to preserve it with modifiers like "the *true* church" is vain. "It is like towing a sinking ship with a canoe."[28]

Nevertheless, he did not entirely give up on it. Thoreau was too seeped in his Puritan heritage for that, or perhaps he had too much faith that the stirring words of the New Testament would one day, like some long forgotten or buried seed, spontaneously spring forth into flowers of truth and beauty. For the church as an institution, he had no hope. But for the *ideal* it sought to represent, he did have hope at some level. "Though every kernel of truth has been carefully swept out of our churches," he wrote, "there yet remains the dust of truth on their walls, so that if you should carry a light into them, they would still, like some powder-mills, blow up at once."[29]

The meetinghouses might even come down without a match, Thoreau also predicted, if the words of Jesus were truly heard in them. There are few books "so truly strange, heretical and unpopular" as the New Testament, he wrote in *A Week*. He then cited examples of Jesus's radical preaching, including his sayings about seeking first the kingdom of heaven, not laying up for oneself treasures on Earth, selling what one has in order to give to the poor, and having the power to move mountains "if ye have faith as a grain of mustard seed."[30]

Think of repeating these things to a New England audience! . . . Who, without cant, can read them aloud? Who, without cant, can hear them, and not go out of the meeting-house? They never were read, they never were heard. Let but one of these sentences be rightly read, from any pulpit in the land, and there would not be left one stone of that meeting-house upon another.[31]

SIX

Rejecting Repentance

Christianity is not the good news it claims to be. That was another central message of *A Week on the Concord and Merrimack Rivers*, and it got Thoreau in as much trouble as his other complaints. By focusing on the corruption of human nature and sin, the church relied on human weakness, not strength. "Let us have institutions framed not out of our rottenness, but out of our soundness," he wrote. The church's emphasis on repentance placed a barrier between humans and God and cast a shadow of despair and resignation over life. Christianity "has hung its harp on the willows, and cannot sing a song in a strange land," Thoreau wrote in *A Week*, alluding to Psalm 137, a lament about the despair of the Israelites in captivity in Babylon. "It has dreamed a sad dream, and does not yet welcome the morning with joy."[1]

Thoreau's comparison of his sin-bowed neighbors to enslaved Israelites may be overdrawn, but other observers have noted the sadness of Puritan culture even decades after the stricter tenants of Calvinism had eased. "The underlying foundation of life in New England was one of profound, unutterable, and therefore unuttered melancholy," Harriet Beecher Stowe wrote in *Oldtown Folks* (1869), her novel about life in Massachusetts in the late eighteenth century. It "regarded human existence itself as a ghastly risk, and, in the case of the vast majority of human beings, an inconceivable misfortune."[2]

For all his criticisms of the Puritans, however, Thoreau shared many of their traits, including their seriousness, abstemious habits, harsh judgments, and tendency toward self-denial. But he drew the line at their notion of humans as mired in sin and in need of redemption. Thoreau did not reject the idea of sin; nor did he see himself without it. In fact, he often confessed his unworthiness, failings, and dereliction of his duty in his *Journal*.

> Now if there are any who think I am vainglorious, that I set myself up above others and crow over their low estate, let me tell them that I could tell a pitiful story respecting myself. . . . I could encourage them with a sufficient list of failures, and could flow as humbly as the very gutters themselves; I could enumerate a list of as rank offenses as ever reached the nostrils of heaven; that I think worse of myself than they can possibly think of me, being better acquainted with the man.[3]

Thoreau said he would retain hope so long as he could command the energy "to take leave of my sin." After recognizing sin, *taking leave of it* was what mattered. The idea that we should wallow in guilt or repent for our fallen nature was repugnant to him. "A wise man will dispense with repentance," he wrote in an undated 1850 *Journal* entry. "It is shocking and passionate. God prefers that you approach him thoughtful, not penitent, though you are the chief of sinners. It is only by forgetting yourself that you draw near to him." It is a mistake, he also wrote, to let our imperfections overwhelm us. "One cannot too soon forget his errors and misdemeanors; for [to] dwell on them is to add to the offense. . . . Not to grieve long for any action, but to go immediately and do freshly and otherwise, subtracts so much from the wrong." Once you have put your hand to the plow of doing right, do not look back.[4]

Thoreau's thoughts on repentance reflect the growing religious liberalism of his day. William Ellery Channing, the pastor of the Federal Street Church in Boston and the uncle of Thoreau's friend and walking companion, Ellery Channing, was the foremost Unitarian theologian and preacher in first two decades of the nineteenth century. In his famous Baltimore Sermon, in 1819, he gave a manifesto for Unitarianism that helped unite and shape the growing movement. In it, he faulted Calvinism for creating a God who is to be dreaded. The purpose of religion, according to Channing, was to ennoble people, not to damn them, to help them have a loving relationship with God, and to realize their moral potential. "We see God around us because God dwells within us," he preached. The Harvard Unitarianism of Thoreau's day similarly recoiled from the wrathful and punishing God of Puritanism.

A difference between Thoreau and Channing, however, is that the latter was a dualist in matters of spirit: the cultivation of the soul was a purely mental act and involved controlling and directing bodily passions to "nobler" ends. Channing wrote in a memoir that he "gained from the Stoics . . . ascetic desires of curbing the animal nature" and of "hardening" himself toward the end of "overcoming effeminacy." As a result, he exhausted his health through punishing hours and physical regimens. Thoreau, in contrast, cultivated his soul without renouncing the body. In *Walden*, he says he admires the Hindu lawgiver who "teaches how to eat, drink, cohabit, void excrement and urine, and the like, elevating what is mean, and does not falsely excuse himself by calling these things trifles."[5]

> Every man is the builder of a temple, called his body, to the god he worships, after a style purely his own, nor can he get off by hammering marble instead. We are all sculptors and painters, and our material is our own flesh and blood and bones.[6]

If Thoreau's views on the subject were not unique in his day, repentance nevertheless touched off an anger in him and stirred some of his most vituperative attacks on the church. "Though you be a babe, the cry is, Repent, repent," he wrote in his *Journal*. "The Christian world will not admit that a man has a just perception of any truth, unless at the same time he cries, 'Lord be merciful to me a sinner.'" He complained about "deadheads" in Concord who were prone to repent. "They fill the churches, and die and revive from time to time. They have nothing to do but sin, and repent of their sins. How can you expect such bloodsuckers to be happy?"[7]

"Of Sick and Diseased Imaginations"

As a schoolboy, Thoreau had to memorize the lesson in *The New England Primer*, "In Adam's fall, we sinned all." As an adult, he turned it on its head. "In the new Adam's rise," he wrote, "we shall all reach the skies." Spending time atoning for the neglect of past opportunities is a waste, he writes in *Walden*. "We loiter in winter while it is already spring. In a pleasant spring morning all men's sins are forgiven."[8]

Thoreau saw repentance as a kind of a self-entanglement that cuts us off from God. Looking back at our failings robs our attention from what we are being given in the present. It prevents us from living every minute with the utmost vitality. "Sin, I am sure, is not in overt acts," he wrote in his *Journal*, "but is in proportion to the time which has come behind us and displaced eternity"—the degree to which we fail to see the numinous and eternal within the ordinary. Sin, then, is a kind of failed attention to the holy. "Woe be to the generation that lets any higher faculty in its midst go unemployed! That is to deny God and know him not." That is not far from the twentieth-century theologian Paul Tillich's famous definition of sin as "a state before it is an act, a state of separation from God." For Thoreau, failed attention separates us from God.[9]

As with his principled refusal to attend church with Ellen Sewell, Thoreau sought to practice his views on repentance. After speaking meanly to Emerson on December 30, 1851, he initially wanted to atone for his behavior, but the next day decided not to repent. "Last night I treated my dearest friend ill," he wrote in his *Journal*. Rather than apologize, Thoreau vowed to act with love and respect toward his friend in the future. "My true relation this instant shall be my apology for my false relation the last instant. I made haste to cast off my injustice as scurf. I own it less than another. I have absolutely done with it. Let the idle and wavering and apologizing friend appropriate it."[10]

The despair Thoreau associated with repentance was a sin against his deep faith in life. It was a refusal, as he wrote in *Walden*, to "obey the hint which God gives them, nor accept the pardon which he freely offers to all."[11]

Churches forget that the hunter wrapped in furs who stands on the edge of the Great Slave Lake does not give up and follow the seal and walrus into the icy waters, Thoreau wrote in first major essay, "A Natural History of Massachusetts," published in 1842, as he was drafting parts of *A Week* into his *Journal*. "The doctrines of despair, of spiritual or political tyranny

or servitude, were never taught by such as shared the serenity
of nature. . . . They are of sick and diseased imaginations who
would toll the world's knell so soon. Cannot these sedentary
sects do better than to prepare the shrouds and write the ep-
itaphs of those other busy living men?" Doctrines of despair
are a form of ingratitude. "Our hymn-books resound with a
melodious cursing of God and enduring Him forever. One
would say that even the prophets and redeemers had rather
consoled the fears than confirmed the hopes of man. There
is nowhere recorded a simple and irrepressible satisfaction
with the gift of life, any memorable praise of God."[12]

Inward Despair and Its Antidote

Thoreau had a striking tendency to associate the church with
death and suicide. In its focus on sin and depravity, it allied
itself with the graveyard and presided over "the funeral of
mankind." Were it not for death and funerals, "I think the institution of the Church would not stand longer," he wrote. The
need to bury the dead—"notwithstanding the danger that they
be buried alive"—would ensure the church's continuance.[13]

Despair touched something deep and dark in Thoreau.
We don't know how much his intermittent bouts of despair,
or "melancholy," lay behind his outbursts at the discourag-
ing news he heard from the church. Thoreau tended to react
stoically to his troubles—his gloom over his failed friendship
with Emerson being a big exception—either by remaining
silent or by forceful exertions to himself to carry on and triumph over them.

Nevertheless, it is possible that he was to a degree pro-
jecting a part of himself onto the church. In a 12-month period from early January 1857 to early January 1858, Thoreau
refers directly to being in despair five times and to suicide

four times. Almost all the references serve as a prelude to a dramatic revival of life and hope, or at least his hope for one, so in a sense the mention of despair becomes a rhetorical foil to his faith in life. Still, the fact that he wrote about the prevalence of despair and thoughts of suicide so often within a year is striking.

On January 13, 1857, the sound of a distant piano lifted him out of a black mood. "We all live a stereotype despair and thus are infidels, do not believe in life," he wrote. "What is there in music that it should so stir our deeps?"

Two days later, he mentioned suicide twice. "We are all ordinarily in a state of desperation; such is our life; oft times it drives us to suicide. To how many, perhaps to most, life is barely tolerable, and if it were not for the fear of death or of dying, what a multitude would immediately commit suicide!" Then comes the rush of hope: "But let us hear a strain of music, we are at once advertised of a life which no man had told us of, which no preacher preaches. . . . The field of my life becomes a boundless plain, glorious to tread, with no death nor disappointment at the end of it. . . . We are actually lifted above ourselves."[14]

In May, Thoreau depicted himself plodding along "in a sort of whitewashed prison entry"—no doubt a recollection of the town jail in which he spent a night in 1846—"subject to some indifferent or even groveling mood. I do not distinctly realize my destiny. I have turned down my light to the merest glimmer and am doing some task which I have set myself. I take incredibly narrow views, live on the limits, and have no recollection of absolute truth. Mushroom institutions hedge me in." Then follows his rescue by a bird. "The voice of eternal wisdom reaches me even, in the strain of the sparrow, and liberates me, whets and clarifies my senses, makes me a competent witness."[15]

On October 31, All Hallows' Eve, Thoreau appeared again to be confronting despair and mentioned laying down to die. The melancholic person, he wrote, should take heart from the buds of the skunk cabbage, which do not shrivel and die as winter approaches.

> If you are afflicted with melancholy at this season, go to the swamp and see the brave spears of skunk-cabbage buds already advanced toward a new year. Their gravestones are not bespoken yet. Who shall be sexton to them? Is it the winter of their discontent? Do they seem to have lain down to die, despairing of skunk-cabbagedom? "Up and at 'em," "Give it to 'em," "Excelsior," "Put it through"—these are their mottos.

Then two days after Christmas, Thoreau again offered advice for the despondent and mentioned suicide. "Do not despair of life. You have no doubt force enough to overcome your obstacles. Think of the fox prowling through wood and field in a winter night for something to satisfy his hunger. Notwithstanding cold and the hounds and traps, his race survives. I do not believe any of them ever committed suicide."

Finally, on January 10, 1858, while visiting the frozen Walden Pond, Thoreau mentioned being in despair for a fifth time. He saw a catkin (the elongated seed) hanging from the branch of an alder tree and felt it might have a dormant life greater than his own. Thoreau's response was not a complaint of insufficiency, however, but an act of faith in nature.

> The north side of Walden is a warm walk in sunny weather. If you are sick and despairing, go forth in winter and see the red alder catkins dangling at the extremities of the twigs, all in the wintry air, like long, hard mulberries, promising a new spring and the fulfillment of all our hopes. We prize

any tenderness, any softening, in the winter—catkins, birds' nests, insect life, etc., etc. The most I get, perchance, is the sight of a mulberry-like red catkin which I know has a dormant life in it, seemingly greater than my own.

The natural world, and the gladness and freedom he found in it, was Thoreau's antidote to despair. "You must converse much with the field and woods, if you would imbibe such health into your mind and spirit as you covet for your body," he wrote. Nature expresses a "naked confidence" not found in the precincts of organized religion. Thoreau was in a marsh in late January 1859, on a bright winter day that seemed to prophesize spring, and hunters were out after muskrats. Thoreau took no pleasure in the killing of any animal, but the zest and naturalness of the hunt stirred a raw love of life in him. The exuberant, innate zeal with which the farmers and their sons pursued the muskrats fulfilled, in its own peculiar way, the Puritan notion of the "chief end of man," which was to glorify God. (He alludes in this passage to clarified butter, a especially refined butter often served at church events.)[16]

I hear these guns going to-day and I must confess they are to me a spring like and exhilarating sound, like the cock crowing, though each one may report the death of a musquash. This, methinks, or the like of this, with whatever mixture of dross, is the real morning or evening hymn that goes up from these vales today, and which the stars echo. This is the best sort of glorifying of God and enjoying him that at all prevails here to-day, without any clarified butter or sacred ladles.[17]

In his late work "The Dispersion of Seeds," Thoreau rejected Psalm 137's association of the willow tree with despair. He told of his joy at discovering that willow twigs, despite being brittle and easily broken off, will take root in a riverbank and sprout into new trees. Unlike the Israelites, who hung their harps on willows "by the waters of Babylon" in despair, Thoreau would hang his harp on a willow on the Concord River in joy at the tree's resilience.

> I do not know what they mean who call the willow the emblem of despairing love—who tell of "the willow worn by forlorn paramour!" It is rather the emblem of triumphant love and sympathy with all Nature. It may droop, it is so lithe, but it never weeps. . . . It is a tree whose ordinary fate it is to be cut down every two or three years, and yet it neither dies nor weeps but puts forth shoots which are all the more vigorous and brighter for it, and it lives as long as most. . . . When I pass by a twig of willow, though of the slenderest kind, rising above the sedge in some dry hollow early in December, or above the snow in midwinter, my spirits rise as if it were an oasis in the desert. . . . Aye, the willow is no tree for suicides. It never despairs. . . . It is the emblem of youth, joy, and everlasting life.[18]

Christianity, Thoreau wrote in *A Week*, "has dreamed a sad dream, and does not yet welcome the morning with joy." The "yet" holds out the slimmest hope that it may reform. But as early as his first book, he was not waiting for that. He created his own rule of life to embrace the good news that Christianity promised but had failed to deliver.

SEVEN

"Dealt With by Superior Powers"

Undergirding both *A Week* and *Walden* are Thoreau's experiences of spiritual rapture in nature. These were moments of awakening that defied what he called the "common laws" of everyday New England Yankee life. They were inklings of a different order of truth that turned ordinary perception upside down. The message that Thoreau heard in the "music" of the telegraph wires along the railroad on January 9, 1853, "stings my ear with everlasting truth," he wrote. "It always intoxicates me, makes me sane, reverses my views of things."[1]

While these moments of union with the ultimate were authoritative for Thoreau, they were also inexpressible. Emerson understood this as well. "Our faith comes in moments; our vice is habitual," he wrote in his essay "The Over-Soul." "Yet there is a depth in those brief moments which constrains us to ascribe more reality to them than to all other experiences." Although such moments were but a fraction of Thoreau's life, they formed a foundation for the rest of it.[2]

"The Innermost Part of My Own Being"

These visitations of spiritual truth came unbidden, Thoreau knew, but he believed certain practices and habits of mind could make him more ready to receive them. The Transcendentalists, translating the notion of *bildung* used by German Romantics, called such efforts self-culture. It was less what Thoreau did—examining a pine cone or a bird nest, communing with frogs in a swamp, reading his beloved classics, or simply sitting in silence—than the attitude with which he did it that cultivated the soul. Chief among these spiritual practices was writing in his *Journal*. In the early 1850s, Thoreau wrote a series of passionate, even fevered, avowals to pursue a higher life that can only be called prayers.

"What more glorious condition of being can we imagine than from [being] impure to becoming pure?" he wrote on July 16, 1851. "That I love and reverence my life! That I am better fitted for a lofty society today than I was yesterday. To make my life a sacrament." He vowed that day to love purity while remembering that he was impure. Despite Thoreau's scorn for Hebraic thought, his many comments about purity match a heightened concern for purity at the center of Jewish religious thought. He also adhered to the link between morality and religion—a Hebrew inspiration.

May I treat myself with more and more respect & tenderness. May I not forget that I am impure & vicious. May I not cease to love purity. May I go to my slumbers as expecting to arise to a new & more perfect day. May I so live and refine my life as fitting myself for a society ever higher than I actually enjoy. May I treat myself tenderly as I would treat the most innocent child whom I love. May I treat children &

my friends as my newly discovered self. Let me forever go in search of myself—never for a moment think that I have found myself. . . . May I be to myself as one is to me whom I love, a dear & cherished object. What temple, what fane [shrine], what sacred place can there be but the innermost part of my own being?

In the spring of 1852, Thoreau burst into a spiritual plea of almost martial intensity. He vowed to persevere and purify himself and to experience his immortality not in the afterlife but now, in the quality of his hours and days—and thus be worthy of what beams of light may fall on him. No Puritan preacher was harder on a wayward parishioner than Thoreau was on himself in his admonishments to strive after purity of soul.

My life partakes of infinity. . . . The air is a velvet cushion against which I press my ear. I go forth to make new demands on life. I wish to begin this summer well—to do something in it worthy of it & of me. To transcend my daily routine & that of my townsmen, to have my immortality now—that it be in the *quality* of my daily life. . . . I pray that the life of this spring and summer may ever lie fair in my memory. May I dare as I have never done. May I persevere as I have never done. May I purify myself anew as with fire & water, soul & body. May my melody not be wanting to the season. May I gird myself to be a hunter of the beautiful, that naught escape me. May I attain to a youth never attained. I am eager to report the glory of the universe— may I be worthy to do it—to have got through with regarding human values so as not to be distracted from regarding divine values.[3]

Thoreau's avowals to grow spiritually continued in midwinter. On Fair Haven Cliff one January, he spied the bud of a buttercup, or "crowfoot," as he called it, nestled in the soil. He imagined the plant to be asleep—yet somehow to hold within it knowledge of a spring the world had yet to see. In his mind's eye, the lowly flower became an Eastern temple, its bud-shaped dome echoing with the fervent prayers of yellow-robed priests.

> It affected me, this tender dome-like bud, within the bosom of the earth, like a temple upon the earth, resounding with the worship of votaries. Methought I saw the flames in yellow robes within it. The crowfoot buds . . . lie unexpanded just beneath the surface. May I lead my life the following year as innocently as they! May it be as fair and smell as sweet! I anticipate nature. Destined to become a fair yellow flower above the surface to delight the eyes of children and its Maker. It offered to my mind a little temple into which to enter and worship.[4]

A "Certain Doubleness"

If Thoreau's spiritual ecstasies gave him a sense of direct access to the divine, his descriptions of them are anything but direct. They seemed to lift him outside of his ordinary life, as suggested by the Greek roots of *ecstasy*, *ek* (out) and *histanai* (to stand or be in stasis). Even in moments of great emotion, Thoreau was sometimes "beside" himself, watching his own experience. He was aware, he wrote in *Walden*, "of a certain doubleness by which I can stand as remote from myself as from another. However intense my experience, I am conscious of the presence and criticism of a part of me, which, as it were, is not a part of me, but a spectator, sharing no experience, but taking note of it."[5]

He told Harrison Blake that he never wholly submitted to his moods but remained always to some extent their critic. One reason is that Thoreau's experiences of heightened perception sometimes prompted gauzy memories or intimations of kind of a prior life or state of consciousness. "As long as I can remember, I have unconsciously referred to the experiences of a previous state of existence," Thoreau wrote in his *Journal*. In *A Week* he wrote of feeling a "sad cheer" at hearing a strain of music that has wafted down to him through the ages, "because we are not one with that which is heard"—that is, with the music at its source.[6]

Thoreau strove for spontaneity and freshness of insight in his *Journal*, so each morning he used the previous day's penciled field notes to write up his encounters in the present tense, as if they were happening as he wrote. His narratives are so convincing that it is hard to believe he was simply recalling what he did the day before. He does not, however, report his mystical moments that way. He imaginatively reconstructs them in past tense, reliving them and creating a secondary experience that sometimes appears to be stronger than the primary one. His exhilaration is paradoxically tinged with melancholy and regret, as he laments that his moments of contact with the beyond have either ended, become too infrequent, or even vanished from his life altogether. His only consolation is his memory of them.

Thoreau often describes himself as spiritually impoverished, compared to the spiritual enrichment of his youth. His journal entry on July 16, 1851, begins with such a self-deprecating declaration. "Methinks my present experience is nothing; my past experience is all in all. I think that no experience which I have today comes up to, or is comparable with, the experiences of my boyhood." Three years later, in 1854, Thoreau was disappointed to feel unmoved by a broad

expanse of the Concord River near Ball's Hill. "This great expanse of deep-blue water, deeper than the sky, why does it not
blue my soul as of yore? . . . The time was when this great blue
scene would have tinged my spirit more." But his reaching
middle age alone did not explain it. He had also felt a lessen-
ing of life's intensity a dozen years earlier, in 1842, when he
was 25. "I can remember when I was more enriched by a few
cheap rays of light falling on the pond-side than by this broad
sunny day," he wrote. "Riches have wings, indeed. . . . When,
in winter, the bees cannot make new honey, they consume
the old."[7]

Such comments, combined with his growing focus on natural phenomena in the 1850s, have contributed to the perception that his later years were marked by spiritual disenchant-
ment and decline. But Thoreau's laments are not to be taken
at face value. He got as discouraged as any human being, but
his complaints about spiritual aridity were more often rhetorical feints and posturing that served to recall, in contrast,
his spiritual raptures. His ecstasies were such a rich, direct
contact with ultimate reality that he missed them as soon as
they ceased. And in any case, as his *Journal* makes abundantly
clear, Thoreau did not cease to have moments of spiritual inspiration in the 1850s.

Nevertheless, there is a histrionic tone of regret about his
spiritual life, as if all that was uplifting had departed from
him. For the final twelve years of his life, Thoreau lived on
the third floor of the family home on Main Street in Concord,
where he often heard his sister Sophia playing piano below.
One day, the inward rhythm of the music, which usually lifted
his spirits, made him feel bereft. I am in the valley, he wrote,
rather than up on Mount Pisgah, viewing the Promised Land.
But the very reference to Moses and the pathos of loss betrays
the melancholic and literary tone of the passage.

I hear the tones of my sister's piano below. It reminds me of strains which once I heard more frequently, when, possessed with the inaudible rhythm, I sought my chamber in the cold and communed with my own thoughts. I feel as if I then received the gifts of the gods with too much indifference. Why did I not cultivate those fields they introduced me to? Does nothing withstand the inevitable march of time? Why did I not use my eyes when I stood on Pisgah? Now I hear those strains but seldom. My rhythmical mood does not endure. I cannot draw from it and return to it in my thought as to a well all the evening or the morning. I cannot dip my pen in it. I cannot work the vein, it is so fine and volatile. Ah, sweet, ineffable reminiscences![8]

Thoreau's attitude about the vicissitudes of the spiritual life could verge on a kind of self-pity, as in his haunting account, written in August 1851, of the plaintive strains of a mysterious musician—identified variously as a clarinetist, flutist, horn player, or singer—heard but not seen in the moonlit woods. The passage is tinged with grief at the loss of the inner music that the mystic alone hears. Thoreau portrayed the imaginary flutist or horn player as his alter ego. He is a man of noble birth who is estranged from his family or has become lost, like the Prodigal Son. The man is "deeply dissatisfied" with his life; he is a slave who yet to discover his true identity and reclaim his royal heritage and his freedom, just as Thoreau hopes to reclaim the ecstatic connection that he had with nature as a child—or even that of just a month earlier, in July! The musician's one redeeming trait is that he faithfully offers his song every night.

I hear now from Bear Garden Hill—I rarely walk by moonlight without hearing—the sound of a flute, or a horn, or a human voice. It is a performer I never see by day; should not recognize him if pointed out; but you may hear his performance in every horizon. He plays but one strain and goes to bed early, but I know by the character of that single strain that he is deeply dissatisfied with the manner in which he spends his day. He is a slave who is purchasing his freedom. He is Apollo watching the flocks of Admetus on every hill, and this strain he plays every evening to remind him of his heavenly descent. It is all that saves him, his one redeeming trait. It is a reminiscence; he loves to remember his youth. He is sprung of a noble family. . . . The elements recognize him, and echo his strain. . . . He is the son of a rich man, of a famous man who served his country well. He has heard his sire's stories. I thought of the time when he would discover his parent age, obtain his inheritance and sing a strain suited to the morning hour. He cherishes hopes. I never see the man by day who plays that clarinet.[9]

The exaggerated sense of loss is typical. Thoreau was influenced by Wordsworth and echoed his elegiac laments over lost emotion and the joys of recollecting them in tranquility. "Our most glorious experiences are a kind of regret," Thoreau wrote. "Our regret is so sublime that we may mistake it for triumph. It is the painful, plaintively sad surprise of our Genius remembering our past lives and contemplating what is possible. . . . It is a regret so divine and inspiring, so genuine, based on so true and distinct a contrast, that it surpasses our proudest boasts and the fairest expectations." Elegy, he wrote in a letter after John's death in 1842, is "some victorious melody or joy escaping from the wreck."[10]

Thoreau had to face the question of how to live in between his moments of spiritual uplift. The distinction between the elevated and the ordinary was clear to him one quiet evening after a hard day's work when he suddenly heard the faithful cricket that had been chirping unheard all day. Were such rare moments so real and true as to cast his ordinary experience into insignificance? Or were they hints of what might yet lie ahead for him?

> In my better hours I am conscious of the influx of a serene and unquestionable wisdom which partly unfits, and if I yielded to it more rememberingly would wholly unfit me, for what is called the active business of life. . . . What is that other kind of life to which I am thus continually allured? Which alone I love? Is it a life for this world? Can a man feed and clothe himself gloriously who keeps only the truth steadily before him? . . . Are our serene moments mere foretastes of heaven—joys gratuitously vouchsafed to us as a consolation—or simply a transient realization of what might be the whole tenor of our lives?[11]

Intoxicated Daily

Despite Thoreau's exaggerated worries about having become spiritually coarse or indifferent—he says in *Walden* that he carries less religion to the table, although that book is shot through with his religious outlook—his spiritual experiences in nature were not in the past, even if they did not attain to the heights of his embellished memories of spiritual enchantment as a youth. In 1857, the sound of a guitar sent him back up Mount Pisgah, where his spirit soared over his own holy land and he experienced "an ecstasy of joy."

> I hear one thrumming a guitar below stairs. It reminds me of moments that I have lived. What a comment on our life is the least strain of music! It lifts me up above all the dust

and mire of the universe. I soar or hover with clean skirts over the field of my life. It is ever life within life, in concentric spheres. The field wherein I toil or rust at any time is at the same time the field for such different kinds of life! The farmer's boy or hired man has an instinct which tells him as much indistinctly, and hence his dreams and his restlessness; hence, even, it is that he wants money to realize his dreams with. The identical field where I am leading my humdrum life, let but a strain of music be heard there, is seen to be the field of some unrecorded crusade or tournament the thought of which excites in us an ecstasy of joy.[12]

Thoreau's contact with nature often resulted in a sudden influx of spirit, or "an emotional elevation and expansion" of the kind William James thought integral to genuine religious experience. Emerson, too, thought enthusiasm usually accompanied consciousness of the divine. "A certain tendency to insanity has always attended the opening of the religious sense in men, as if they had been 'blasted with excess of light,'" Emerson wrote in "The Over-Soul." Thoreau recorded many instances of being so blasted, but none more beautiful than the one he wrote to conclude his effusive, 2,700-word *Journal* entry on July 16, 1851, the very same day he mourned that his present experience was "nothing." Thoreau's "heavenly pleasures" that day were delivered to him by senses, but he did not believe he begot them by his own initiative. Underscoring the relational or "I-Thou" character of his religious thought, he described them as benign "interference" in his life by "superior powers." He alluded to this by speaking in dialogue.[13]

This earth was the most glorious musical instrument, and I was audience to its strains. To have such sweet impressions made on us, such ecstasies begotten of the breezes! I can remember how I was astonished. I said to my self, I said to others, "There comes into my mind such an indescribable, infinite, all-absorbing, divine, heavenly pleasure, a sense of elevation and expansion, and [I] have had nought to do with it. I perceive that I am dealt with by superior powers. This is a pleasure, a joy, an existence which I have not procured myself. I speak as a witness on the stand, and tell what I have perceived." The morning and the evening were sweet to me, and I led a life aloof from society of men. . . . The maker of me was improving me. When I detected this interference I was profoundly moved. For years I marched as to a music in comparison with which the military music of the streets is noise and discord. I was daily intoxicated, and yet no man could call me intemperate. With all your science can you tell how it is, and whence it is, that light comes into the soul?

"Surely joy is the condition of life," Thoreau famously wrote. It is a declarative statement, but the modifier *surely* preserves just the slightest edge of doubt for a man who could never quite be sure of his good fortune at being alive and knowing the wonders of the natural world. But I think there would have been no qualifier in Thoreau's agreement with the French philosopher and scientist Teilhard de Chardin, who said joy is the infallible sign of the presence of God.[14]

EIGHT

A Pantheon with
an Open Roof

The wobbly structure of *A Week* drew perhaps the most critical fire when it was published in 1849, with the acerbic critic James Russell Lowell comparing its lengthy philosophical digressions and verses to a canoe hitting rocks and snags. But readers were also greatly troubled by the book's impiety. Horace Greeley spoke for many of them when, in his review in the *New York Tribune*, which appeared two weeks after the book's publication, he called it a "misplaced Pantheistic attack on the Christian faith." Today, interest in earth-centered religions is one of the biggest developments in American religion, but back then the pantheist label was flung as an accusation.[1]

While there is no single form of pantheism, in general a pantheist believes that nature is sacred in and of itself. *Pan* is Greek for "everything." In pantheism the divine is the totality of the natural world; there is no distinction between them. Generally speaking, pantheism is the theology of modern paganism. There are at least two reasons to put Thoreau in that camp. First, some of his most inspired prose portrays a natural world aflame with spirit. Second, in the conclusion to *A Week*, Thoreau clearly says that nature is itself the thing for which it is taken to be a symbol—that is, God.

The problem is, over the next few pages, Thoreau also provides clear evidence that he regards nature as less than that for which it is taken to be the symbol. And he will periodically assert the symbolic nature of natural facts and refer to a source of mystery beyond or through them for the rest of his life.

The scholar Bron Taylor sees Thoreau as an early exemplar of what he calls "dark green religion." By that term, he means "religion that considers nature to be sacred, imbued with intrinsic value, and worthy of reverent care. Dark green religion considers nonhuman species to have worth, regardless of their usefulness to human beings. Such religion expresses and promotes an ethics of kinship between human beings and other life forms." I think that is correct, and that Thoreau did hold, for example, animist and pantheist beliefs. But he was no more definite and no more consistent about such beliefs than he was about any other aspect of religion. And however expansively one interprets pantheism, it does not square with the many times Thoreau, in his *Journal* and published writings, portrays God and nature as ontologically distinct. Thoreau does refer to worshipping stones and describes natural objects as sacred, but his consistently stated position is that Walden Pond and the pickerel and bream in it—as well as trees, wildflowers, rainbows, and other natural objects—are images or emanations of God, rather than divine in and of themselves.[2]

Many interpreters have also seen Thoreau as an agnostic religious humanist. It true that he never declared a belief in a transcendent God in a clear, propositional way. But such a view goes against his negative opinion of human nature, the minor role humanity holds in his scheme of things, his higher regard for the wild, nonhuman world, and his view of the universe as a divine creation. Thoreau climbed Fair Haven Hill in order to "see the forms of the mountains in the horizon—to behold and commune with something grander than man." He complained that our books are too human centered because they exclude the "fresh views of nature" that animals would offer if only they could write. He inveighed against excessive morality, which he called a "jaundice reflected from man." It is hard to imagine a humanist writing the following, as Thoreau did on January 3, 1853:[3]

> I love Nature partly because she is not man, but a retreat from him. None of his institutions control or pervade her. There a different kind of right prevails. In her midst I can be glad with an entire gladness. If this world were all man, I could not stretch myself, I should lose all hope. He is constraint, she is freedom to me. He makes me wish for another world. She makes me content with this. . . . What he touches he taints. In thought he moralizes.

Thoreau did not call himself a pantheist and only tentatively accepted the label when Greeley applied it to him a second time, in 1853. Greeley, who acted as Thoreau's literary patron, was exasperated to learn that *Putnam's Magazine* had found sections of an essay Thoreau submitted blasphemous. "Don't you see," he wrote Thoreau, the need to eliminate "very flagrant heresies (like your defiant Pantheism)?" Although he thanked Greeley for his help, Thoreau replied petulantly that the "mangling" of his manuscript could not be helped, "since I was born to be a pantheist—if that be the name of me—and do the deeds of one."[4]

Another but less justifiable reason Thoreau might be called

a pantheist is his famous, and misunderstood, declaration of fidelity to the Greek god Pan in *A Week*. In the "Monday" chapter, Thoreau puns that Pan, the shaggy shepherd god, reigns in his "Pantheon." He also declares himself "most constant" at the god's shrine. Thoreau loved Greek myth and religion, and the bearded, old, flute-playing Pan surely appealed to him more than the "angry God" in whose hands Jonathan Edwards imagined sinners dangling. But Thoreau was not defining his faith in this classical reference. He had just called Christianity a new myth, and his purpose is to show that the Christian God is one among many personalities of God, including those of Greek myth, and that the Christian version is no more or less valid than the others. As for the constancy of Thoreau's devotion to Pan, he never mentioned the Greek god again in his *Journal*, letters, or published works. Indeed, the single mention of Pan in his *Journal* is on December 25, 1841 ("Pan himself lives in the wood"). After that, Pan mysteriously disappears from Thoreau's pantheon.[5]

"May We Not See God?"

The more compelling and frequently cited argument for Thoreau's pantheism is his assertion in *A Week* that nature is not merely a symbol or emblem of higher truths. "We need pray for no higher heaven than the pure senses can furnish, a *purely* sensuous life," he declares in the "Friday" chapter. Thoreau's wordplay muddles his meaning. He soon makes clear that by "pure senses" and a "*purely* sensuous life" he does not mean pure sensuality, but rather senses that have been cleansed and purified to behold the unseen and the unheard. "Our present senses are but the rudiments of what they are destined to become," he writes. Our eyes and ears "were not made for such groveling uses as they are now put to" but "to hear celestial sounds" and "to behold beauty now invisible." He then famously asks:

> May we not see God? Are we to be put off and amused in this life, as it were with a mere allegory? Is not Nature, rightly read, that of which she is commonly taken to be the symbol merely?[6]

Thoreau is rejecting an allegory or dualism that separates nature and divinity. Seen with the eyes of the heart, they are one. To perceive this reality, Thoreau says, we need "not only to be spiritualized, but *naturalized*." But he never suggests that nature exhausts or contains the divine. The sacred for Thoreau is here and now, and it is also beyond the range of sound and verge of sight. It is not a case of either/or for him, but one of both/and. The same passage continues:[7]

> When the common man looks into the sky . . . he thinks it less gross than the earth, and with reverence speaks of "the Heavens," but the seer will in the same sense speak of "the Earths," and his Father who is in them. "Did not he that made that which is within, make that which is without also?" What is it, then, to educate but to develop these divine germs called the senses?[8]

The quote is Luke 11:40, "Ye fools, did not he that made that which is without make that which is within also?" The maker of the world, Thoreau is saying, is the maker of the soul within us. The natural world is not *merely* a symbol, because the divine is plowed into and through creation. A "creative genius" is at work in nature. We cannot, however, front this miraculous fact directly. To know it even partially we must turn our explorations inward. This is not easy, he acknowledges. "It is easier to discover another such a new world as Columbus did, than to go within one fold of this which we appear to know so well." Still, we may yet hope to discover it, for it only takes a moment's sanity and sound senses "to teach us that there is a nature behind the ordinary." We may have a vague sense of this spirit land, but we do not own it and may not enter it in ordinary prosaic consciousness. "We live on the outskirts of that region."[9]

What Thoreau is doing in *A Week* is locating the divine in the natural world while preserving a sense of transcendence. His assertion of this "nature behind the ordinary" is not a philosophical or logical conclusion. It is borne out of his amazement and wonder that we are surrounded by beauty in a world that is not of our making. His openness to transcendence was a profound and humble gratitude for the gift of life, which he saw as originating from a source beyond the sensory world. Indeed, Thoreau's gratitude for his life was another strand in his spirituality, as he disclosed in a letter to Blake.

I am grateful for what I am and have. My thanksgiving is perpetual. It is surprising how contented one can be with nothing definite—only a sense of existence. Well, anything for variety. I am ready to try this for the next ten thousand years, and exhaust it. How sweet to think of! My extremities well charred, and my intellectual part, too, so that there is no danger of worm or rot for a long while. My breath is sweet to me. O how I laugh when I think of my vague, indefinite riches. No run on my bank can drain it, for my wealth is not possession but enjoyment.[10]

Thoreau would devote the last decade of his life to seeing the natural world on its own terms and to an exacting study of its processes and rhythms. He spoke less often of its symbolic value as he sought to move beyond the Emersonian theory of correspondence, which was largely based on the views of Emanuel Swedenborg and which saw the natural world as a system of signs representing the spiritual. But Thoreau's openness to materiality did not mean he ceased looking for the fact to flower into a truth or to see "the significance of phenomena." His idealism became more grounded as he sought ever closer contact with the natural world, but it never disappeared. He continued to turn at times to nature as a language for expressing what was deepest in him. As late as 1860, Thoreau could refer to "the physical fact which in all language is the symbol of the spiritual."[11]

On Christmas Day 1851, Thoreau was enchanted by a crimson sunset. A merely phenomenal description of it, he wrote, would "rob it of its symbolicalness" and impoverish his experience of it.

> It is what it suggests and is the symbol of that I care for, and if, by any trick of science, you rob it of its symbolicalness, you do me no service and explain nothing. . . . This red vision excites me, stirs my blood, makes my thoughts flow, and I have new and indescribable fancies, and you have not touched the secret of that influence. . . . What sort of science is that which enriches the understanding, but robs the imagination?

Thoreau denies being a "true idealist" in *Walden*, but in his mystical moods he sounds like one and sides more with Plato than with Aristotle in the classic debate between idealism and empiricism. Indeed, as we saw in chapter 4, the "actual" was less real to him than the spiritual truths he discerned via intuition. Actual events, he wrote in 1850, "notwithstanding the singular prominence which we all allow them, are far less real than the creations of my imagination."[12]

"Man cannot afford to be a naturalist, to look at Nature directly, but only with the side of his eye," Thoreau wrote in 1853. "He must look through and beyond her. To look at her is as fatal as to look at the head of Medusa. It turns the man of science to stone." Even a humble fungus could appear to him as the expression of an idea. "There is suggested something superior to any particle of matter, in the idea or mind which uses and arranges the particles."[13]

On the other hand, to arrange the particles or to perceive the "idea" behind them too quickly was to risk letting preconceptions or inherited views block a direct and fresh contact with natural facts, which was his aim. "Ah give me pure mind—pure thought. Let me not be in haste to detect the universal law, let me see more clearly a particular instance." Such direct seeing disclosed the spiritual for Thoreau.[14]

Thoreau disagreed that the natural world exists to serve human purposes. But he did not believe the corollary—that in order to perceive it truly we must remove any human interpretation of, or relationship, to it. "A history of animated nature must itself be animated," he wrote on February 18, 1860. A fact, he wrote five days later, "must be the vehicle of some humanity in order to interest us," to stir our desire to learn from the natural world and our compassion to protect and preserve it.

The "Last of Nature" and "First of God"

In May 1854, Thoreau saw a beautiful red bird, likely a tanager. At first he imagined that the deeper woods held an even redder, wilder bird than the one he saw that day. But he soon decided that nature would not match his imagination. God, he concluded, begins where nature ends.

> We soon get through with Nature. She excites an expecta-
> tion which she cannot satisfy. . . . The red-bird which I saw
> on my companion's string on election days I thought but the
> outmost sentinel of the wild, immortal camp—of the wild
> and dazzling infantry of the wilderness—that the deeper
> woods abounded with redder birds still; but, now that I have
> threaded all our woods and waded the swamps, I have never
> yet met with his compeer, still less his wilder kindred. The
> red-bird which is the last of Nature is the first of God.[15]

There is a twenty-five-foot opening in the dome of the Pantheon in Rome called an oculus, from the Latin for "eye"—the only source of natural light in the rotund temple. It may also have been intended as a portal through which the gods could pass. Whether or not Pan "reigned" in his own "Pantheon," Thoreau suggested that his tower to the gods was open at the top.

NINE

Thoreau's God

If Thoreau was not a pantheist, what was he? No label suffices, but Thoreau encountered and wrote about that transcendent divine source that people throughout history have called God. His God was an infinite, life-giving presence manifest in the natural world and yet not contained by it. It was a God of wildness, surprise, and change, yet it was at the same time benign and loving. Thoreau accepted this divine mystery as the central if unknowable reality of his life, and sought communion with it. In moments of ecstasy he wrote with an emotional certainty about this source, but his belief in a personal God was contingent, never final, more of a moving toward than an arriving at. However tentative his conviction, his fleeting glimpses and tastes of the divine deeply moved him and fueled his religious imagination.

Thoreau's ideas about God evolved from the more personal theism of his early writing to God as an organic creative force and source of moral law, as evinced in *Walden*, to a more integrative conception of divinity in the later 1850s that merged the mystical and the material. But such differences were of degrees rather than large shifts. Thoreau's theological thought also did not evolve in a straight line. His earliest writings have passages in which his consciousness is mystically identified with natural processes, and his later writings are punctuated by what Lawrence Buell has called his "pop-up theism," or references to a personal creator, which continue to appear as late as 1861, when Thoreau wrote the abolitionist minister Parker Pillsbury, "Blessed are they who never read a newspaper, for they shall see Nature, and, through her, God."[1]

Thoreau was, predictably, inconsistent in expressing his theology. He sometimes spoke in diffuse Emersonian terms about an impersonal, abstract divine mind or soul in nature. It was, Thoreau said, the "Universal Intelligence" or "the spirit itself which resides in these woods," or the "divine mind" that writes its thoughts in the tracks on the frozen pond in winter. In spring, the melting Walden Pond had "intelligence with some remote horizon." "Nature is full of genius, full of the divinity." In Thoreau's experiences of spiritual rapture in nature, the walls that normally separated him from the divine at times dissolved, and he was one with it. "Emersonianism," as William James described such an idealist theology, "seems to let God evaporate into abstract Ideality. . . . Not a deity *in concreto*, not a superhuman person, but the immanent divinity in things, the essentially spiritual structure of the universe."[2]

"The Greater Benefactor and Intelligence"

But Thoreau also consistently drew on his inherited religious frameworks to conceive of a creator God who was both immanent in nature and its indefinite, transcendent source. This was not the distant God of deism, remote from the world it spun into being. Thoreau speaks of a divine mystery to which he feels personally related—"the great secret of my life," an unseen, cosmic force at the core his being. He gives fullest expression to that view in *Walden*, indeed making the pond a symbol of God. In *A Week*, Thoreau struggles with how to divorce the religious sentiment from its institutional context. By *Walden*, the bulk of which he wrote after 1849, he has figured it out. Transcendence is woven through its vision of the natural world. It is a theological vision, although not a systematic one, about a creative force beyond nature. "We strive to retain and increase the divinity in us when the greater part of divinity is out of us," he wrote in his *Journal* six weeks after moving to the pond. In the chapter "Solitude," he wrote, "Nearest to all things is that power which fashions their being. Next to us the grandest laws are continually being executed. Next to us is not the workman whom we have hired, with whom we love so well to talk, but the workman whose work we are."[3]

And in the conclusion, he delights to "walk even with the Builder of the Universe," which helps him "come to my bearings."

> As I stand over the insect crawling amid the pine needles on the forest floor, and endeavoring to conceal itself from my sight, and ask myself why it will cherish those humble thoughts, and hide its head from me who might, perhaps, be its benefactor, and impart to its race some cheering information, I am reminded of the greater Benefactor and Intelligence that stands over me the human insect.[4]

The Scottish biographer of Thoreau, Alexander Hay Japp, was among the first to emphasize his spirituality. The lesson of Transcendentalism, Japp wrote, is the same whether exemplified by a Christian mystic like Meister Eckhart or by Thoreau. "All life is sanctified by the relation in which it is seen to the source of life—an idea which lies close to the Christian spirit." Thoreau spoke plainly of being in relation to such a source in a letter to Harry Blake. "I believe something, and there is nothing else but that," he wrote his Worcester friend and disciple in 1848. "I know that I am. I know that another is who knows more than I, who takes interest in me, whose creature, and yet whose kindred, in one sense, am I. I know that the enterprise is worthy. I know that things work well. I have heard no bad news."[5]

A Kind of Holy Ignorance

When it came to proving God's existence, however, Thoreau was uninterested. Apologies for God showed bad faith, he thought. He also seemed to believe that elaborate arguments were needed only to underpin or prove a dubious assertion or a misconception, whereas the truth stands naked and alone quite well. "It is remarkable," he writes, "that almost all speakers and writers feel it to be incumbent on them, sooner or later, to prove or to acknowledge the personality of God. Some Earl of Bridgewater, thinking it better late than never, has provided for it in his will. It is a sad mistake." In that remark Thoreau is dismissing the form, or personality, into which God is put—not the Godhead or divine principle it is meant to represent. He often uses qualifiers, such as "my country's God," to indicate that he is speaking of the deity whom he sees as a projection of human notions of authority and respectability. With a wink, he calls the clergy "men of God, *so-called*" and says the *Protestant* God is too stern (emphasis added).[6]

But the true God, he writes in *A Week*, is something else. "The perfect God in his revelations of himself has never got to the length of one such proposition as you, his prophets, state." All the gods ever worshipped have been men, Thoreau wrote in his *Journal* in 1849, "but of the true God of whom none have conceived, all men combined would hardly furnish the germ." The important words in that sentence are "of whom none have conceived." Thoreau's knowledge of God was mystical. It drew on a kind of holy ignorance or, as the anonymous fourteenth-century English monk wrote in his handbook on contemplative prayer, a blind thrust through "a cloud of unknowing." Thoreau repeatedly asserts that God is unfathomable mystery, like the secret concealed in the snowy wood that he walked through on January 30, 1841, which I mentioned in chapter 1. The long rows of trees embowered by snow suggested the aisles of a cathedral. "You are never so far in them as they are far before you," Thoreau wrote of the trees. "Their secret is where you are not and where your feet can never carry you."[7]

Calling Out the Morning Light

Who is this "true God" of whom Thoreau speaks, this "another" whom he mentions in his letter to Blake, "whose creature, and yet whose kindred" he feels that he is? Thoreau's standard answer is not to give one, just as, in *Walden*, he lets the silent dawning sun be the unspoken answer one morning to a question he had been puzzling over in his sleep. Thoreau does not refer to the negative or apophatic theology of mysticism, but he adheres to its belief that we can never say what God *is*, only what God *is not*. "The divinity is so fleeting," he wrote in his *Journal*, "that its attributes are never expressed." Thoreau did not mean that the divinity itself is fleeting, but rather that our perception or glimpses of it are.[8]

Thoreau's writing nevertheless does provide clues to his understanding of God. The summer of 1851 was a period of heightened awareness during which scholars believe Thoreau crystallized his life's mission. On September 7, he pledged to find God in nature. This often-cited passage is a not a creed or statement of belief, but a pledge to pay attention, to notice, to be awake. Seeing with the eyes of the soul was at the heart of Thoreau's religion, as it was for John Calvin, who despite his views on predestination made perception an essential part of his theology. Seeing aright was also key to the religious thought of Edwards and Emerson.

> If by watching all day and all night I may detect some trace of the Ineffable, then will it not be worth the while to watch? . . . If by patience, if by watching I can secure one new ray of light, can feel myself elevated for an instant upon Pisgah [the mountain from which Moses glimpsed the Promised Land], the world which was dead prose to me become living and divine, shall I not watch ever? Shall I not be a watchman henceforth? If by watching a whole year on the city's walls I may obtain a communication from heaven, shall I not do well to shut up my shop and turn a watchman? . . . To watch for, describe, all the divine features which I detect in Nature. . . . My profession is to be always on the alert to find God in nature, to know his lurking places. To attend all the oratorios, the operas in nature.

Thoreau uses some form of the word *watch* nine times within a 450-word section of this long entry—an allusion to the watchman who calls out the morning light, a recurring motif in the Psalms. Thoreau was often out at 4 a.m. to greet the dawn and call it out to those of us who read his *Journal* today.[9]

Thoreau did find God in the beauty and harmony of the natural world—in the breezes that rippled Walden Pond, the sonorous vibrations of church bells, the gemlike colors of a pickerel, the lacy sheaves of ice in a frosted window, the buds that swell in spring, and the leaves in autumn that teach us how to die. "The calling of Jonathan Edwards was not more full of sweet and quiet rapture," said John Weiss, his Harvard classmate, referring to the eighteenth-century divine who read the landscape as a sacred text. Despite Edwards's more famous hellfire sermons, the Puritan also detected the "signs and wonders" of God in thunderstorms, spiderwebs, trees, rivers, and the shapes of clouds. Edwards described walking in his father's pasture as a boy. "And as I was walking there, and looking upon the sky and clouds, there came into my mind so sweet a sense of the glorious majesty and grace of God, as I know not how to express."[10]

"The Almighty Is Wild above All"

Thoreau was similar to Edwards in seeing nature as revelation, but their theology still differed. Thoreau experienced God not only in sweet "signs and wonders" but also in the claw and tooth of nature, in its chaos, decay, and predation, in the storms that level forests, the waves that crush ships, and the wild dive of a hawk at its prey. Thoreau saw a radical otherness and transformative wildness in God. It was the ungovernable and inexhaustible spirit of life itself, and it was holy. "There is in my nature, methinks, a singular yearning toward all wildness," Thoreau wrote in *A Week*. To connect with wildness is to be fully human. "The most alive is the wildest," he wrote in "Walking." The wild, as Thoreau conceived of it, is a generative, renewing, and liberating force that is both in us and at the same time is larger than us. It emanates from a source beyond us and will go on without us. "The Almighty is wild above all," Thoreau wrote in his *Journal*. In 1846, he climbed Mount Katahdin, where he encountered a "primeval, untamed, forever untamable" power over which humans have no control. Thoreau felt chastened that day, as if he had trespassed into nature's innermost sanctum. But when he wrote about his ascent back in Concord, he described the raw, weather-beaten summit as a sacred place—"a specimen of what God saw fit to make this world." Thoreau believed that we align ourselves to God when we reverence our wild nature.[11]

"Ah, bless the Lord, O my soul! bless him for wildness," Thoreau wrote in a playful recasting of Psalm 104, "for crows that will not alight within gunshot! And bless him for hens, too, that croak and cackle in the yard!"[12]

John Muir, who was deeply influenced by his reading of Thoreau, also believed in the salvific power of wildness. When Muir wrote, in 1890, "In God's wildness lies the hope of the world," he may have had in mind Thoreau's famous dictum, in "Walking": "In Wildness is the preservation of the world." Wildness remains redemptive for Thoreau so long as it does not become so tamed or "civilized" as to lose its power to refresh the world. "Give me a wildness no civilization can endure," he also wrote in "Walking."[13]

A corollary to Thoreau's understanding of wildness is that he could not abide the view some Puritans held of the woods outside their "plantations" as the precincts of the devil and a den of lust and sin. "Generally speaking, a howling wilderness does not howl," Thoreau wrote with his usual dry humor in *The Maine Woods*, alluding to Cotton Mather's description of the woods around Puritan towns. "It is the imagination of the traveler that does the howling."[14]

"What shall we do with a man who is afraid of the woods, their solitude and darkness?" he also asked in his *Journal*. "What salvation is there for him? God is silent and mysterious."[15]

The "Scene-Shifter"

God was also "the Scene-shifter" for Thoreau, a God of surprises, a God of creativity, and a God in motion, as dynamic as the forces that ceaselessly remake the earth. In this, Thoreau's thought also looks back to Edwards's emphasis on God's generativity. As the only true substance and only true cause, Edwards believed, God essentially recreates the universe every moment. "God is a pure act," he said. Thoreau saw God as the originative element or life force animating the universe and repairing its entropy and decay. In that sense, Thoreau's thought looks forward at the same time to aspects of twentieth-century process theology, which emphasizes the dynamism and mutability of God. Two months after his brother, John, died, Thoreau reflected on the two elemental forces in the world—a view central to the philosophy of Alfred North Whitehead, a founder of process theology.[16]

> There seem to be two sides to this world, presented us at
> different times, as we see things in growth or dissolution,
> in life or death. For seen with the eye of a poet, as God sees
> them, all are alive and beautiful; but seen with the historical
> eye, or the eye of the memory, they are dead and offensive.
> If we see Nature as pausing, immediately all mortifies and
> decays; but seen as progressing, she is beautiful.[17]

In his junior year at Harvard, Thoreau had a course in natural theology, which was a religious reaction to the Enlightenment that sought to justify Christianity according to the rational methods of eighteenth-century natural science. In his treatise *Natural Theology* (1802), the English clergyman and apologist William Paley held that the intricate design of nature proves that God made the world, as a watch must

have a watchmaker. Thoreau was unimpressed. He was more
concerned with God's presence in nature today, not in ages
past. His theology was in his geology. At Harvard Thoreau also
read Charles Lyell's *Principles of Geology*, published between
1830 and 1833, which overturned the prevailing view that the
earth was like a rigid fossil cast by cataclysms eons ago. Lyell
showed that Earth was shaped by natural processes that are
still active and ongoing today—an idea that thrilled Thoreau
and confirmed his own experience. "The earth I tread on is
not a dead, inert mass," he wrote on December 31, 1851. "It is
a body, has a spirit, is organic, and fluid to the influence of its
spirit, and to whatever particle of that spirit is in me. She is
not dead, but sleepeth."

Thoreau also associated those internal natural forces with
God—while making clear that he accepted the evolutionary
dynamic of the so-called development theory that was emerging from the work of Darwin and others in the natural sci-
ences. In *Walden*, in his famous passage about the railroad
sandbank that he calls the Deep Cut, Thoreau sees the moist,
lobe-shaped rivulets of gravely sand extruding from the bank
as evidence that the original moment of creation is ongoing.
"On the outside all the life of the earth is expressed in the
animal or vegetable, but make a deep cut in it, and you find
it vital," he wrote in the original *Journal* entry from which
the *Walden* passage was taken. The sandbank was proof,
as it were, that the earth is a furnace and that "nature is 'in
full blast' within." In the molten mass Thoreau sees a divine
smithy strewing about new matter and forms. "There is nothing inorganic," he writes, stating a central theme of *Walden* in
four words.[18]

I am affected as if in a peculiar sense I stood in the labora-
tory of the Artist who made the world and me—had come to

where he was still at work, sporting on this bank, and with excess of energy strewing his fresh designs about.[19]

A God in Motion

Thoreau associated God with other kinds of movement and flow in nature. He detected the divine presence in swaying trees, driving surf, and waves of sound, including, and perhaps especially, music. He characterized a moment of ecstasy as "a perpetual flow of spirit," replete with stamping steeds and prancing knights.

> A thrumming of piano-strings beyond the gardens and through the elms. At length the melody steals into my being. I know not when it began to occupy me. By some fortunate coincidence of thought or circumstance I am attuned to the universe, I am fitted to hear. My being moves in a sphere of melody, my fancy and imagination are excited to an inconceivable degree. This is no longer the dull earth on which I stood. It is possible to live a grander life here; already the steed is stamping, the knights are prancing; already our thoughts bid a proud farewell to the so-called actual life and its humble glories. Now this is the verdict of a soul in health. . . . This suggests what a perpetual flow of spirit would produce.[20]

On Heywood's Peak, a tall ridge on the north shore of Walden Pond, Thoreau saw a flock of birds fly over the pond. The graceful rippling of their wings led him to think that the subtlest and "most ideal" spiritual motion is undulation. "If you consider it from the hilltop, you will detect it [undulation] in the wings of birds endlessly repeated. The two waving lines which express flight seem copied from the ripple. There is something analogous to this in our most inward experience. In enthusiasm we undulate to the divine *spiritus*, as the lake to the wind."[21]

Undulating to the *divine spiritus* like a bird in flight or experiencing the divine in the beauty and wildness of nature was one thing. Representing that experience in words was something else. There was an inherent tension between Thoreau's mystical religious outlook and his vocation as an artist whose medium was words. This was especially true when it came to naming God.

TEN

To "Fable the Ineffable"

Thoreau was ambivalent about the word *God*. It was tarnished by starchy piety and conveyed too much certainty about something he saw as ineffable, or that which that surpasses the capacity of language to express it. *Ineffable* is from the Latin *ineffabilis*, "unutterable," and Thoreau took that literally at times. In letter to Harry Blake in 1850, he wrote that, just as we might lie on the lap of Earth to rest our bodies, "so, when we would rest our spirits, we must recline on the Great Spirit." When we let things alone, "God reigns." But then Thoreau appeared to think twice about using *God*.

> Let God alone if need be. Methinks, if I loved him more, I should keep him—I should keep myself rather—at a more respectful distance. It is not when I am going to meet him, but when I am just turning away and leaving him alone, that I discover that God is. I say, God. I am not sure that that is the name. You will know whom I mean.[1]

It is remarkable that, despite such concerns, *God*, upper-
case, appears more than 200 times in the Princeton edition
of Thoreau's *Journal*, in the published volumes and online
transcripts, excluding editorial matter and common expressions ("God's sake," "God-speed") and very incidental uses.
Thoreau referred to the idea of God many more times if one
includes his creative appellations such as "the great artist,"
"the Maker," "maker of the Universe," "the highest," and "Universal Intelligence." The number of such references means
nothing by itself. *God* was part of the furniture of the mind in
Thoreau's culture, and many of his uses of it are pro forma,
rote, or even sarcastic, as when he mocks the speech of un-
bearably pious persons or says facetiously, "Thank God, they
cannot cut down the clouds." However, it is fair to say that in
the majority of times, Thoreau is speaking about God without
cant or question. And a smaller but still significant number
of his references to the deity stand out as thoughtful, delib-
erate, and poignant speech about a benevolent, friendly, but
also disorienting presence that Thoreau seeks to know, wonders about, is shaken by, derives happiness from, or thrills to
experience.[2]

Thoreau's references to God can be hard to interpret. On
June 22, 1852, a series of thunderstorms in Concord were followed by a rainbow at sunset, reminding him how "moral"
the world is made. The rainbow is not utilitarian, Thoreau
wrote.

> After the rain he sets his bow in the heavens! The world
> is not destitute of beauty. . . . While men cultivate flowers
> below, God cultivates flowers above—he takes charge of the
> parterres [pastures] in the heavens. Is not the rainbow a
> faint vision of God's face? How glorious should be the life of
> man passed under this arch!

The pastoral imagery and wordplay points to a poetic use of the term *God*. But the earnest tone suggests otherwise, and it seems unlikely that so disciplined and gifted a writer as Thoreau would use a metaphor that meant nothing to him. Thoreau also seems to be drawing on God's declaration in Genesis 9:13: "I do set my bow in the cloud, and it shall be for a token of a covenant between me and the earth." And when Thoreau recalled the rainbow six weeks later, his comment further suggests that he was being earnest. "What form of beauty could be imagined more striking and conspicuous? An arch of the most brilliant and glorious colors completely spanning [the] heavens before the eyes of men. . . . Plainly thus the maker of the Universe sets the seal to his covenant with men."[3]

One can make too much of Thoreau's references to God, but one can make too little of them as well. Thoreau was not someone who used words carelessly or because others used them. One of the stumbling blocks to seeing Thoreau as religious is a tendency to think he cannot possibly mean what he says—that, given his opposition to formal religion and his nature piety, there must be some rhetorical finesse or hidden meaning in his speech about God that defies the common-sense interpretation. I would argue that Thoreau means what he says. I do not doubt whom Thoreau was addressing when he wrote, "Thou art a personality so vast and universal that I have never seen one of thy features." I believe he felt humbled by something beyond himself when he said, "I perceive I am dealt with by superior powers."[4]

Indeed, the word *God* doesn't really matter at all. One of Thoreau's most poignant expressions of faith is in *A Week*.

> I see, smell, taste, hear, feel, that everlasting Something
> to which we are allied, at once our maker, our abode, our

destiny, our very Selves; the one historic truth, the most remarkable fact which can become the distinct and uninvited
subject of our thought, the actual glory of the universe; the
only fact which a human being cannot avoid recognizing, or
in some way forget or dispense with.[5]

Thoreau here does not identify "Something" as God; he
does not have to. It is the divine principle that matters to
him, not the name, and the passage may have more rhetorical force without it. Nevertheless, it is worth noting that the
preceding sentence in *A Week* is: "Heal yourselves, doctors;
by God, I live."

Ferried to a "Newer World"

Thoreau's references to God do not to prove he was a confirmed theist. I cite them because the amount and quality of
his speech about God appears to be little known, certainly
in comparison to other aspects of his religious thought. And
however limited such references to God may be to understanding Thoreau, they do reveal the depth of his religiosity
and his yearning for the infinite and eternal.

Thoreau's most sustained poetic description of a transcendent God is in *Cape Cod*, in a moving tribute to the 145 Irish
immigrants who perished in the wreck of the *St. John* off Co-
hasset, in 1849. In atypical but still Protestant terms, Thoreau
makes God a pilot who invisibly ferries the souls of the dead
to halcyon shores as their drowned bodies tumble in the surf.
In a play on the term the *New World*, Thoreau sends the dead
to a "newer world" that science has not yet discovered—but of
whose existence there is more "convincing evidence" than for
the actual continent Columbus claimed:

Their owners were coming to the New World, as Columbus and the Pilgrims did—they were within a mile of its shores; but before they could reach it, they emigrated to a newer world than ever Columbus dreamed of, yet one of whose existence we believe that there is far more universal and convincing evidence—though it has not yet been discovered by science—than Columbus had of this; not merely mariners' tales and some paltry drift-wood and sea-weed, but a continual drift and instinct to all our shores. I saw their empty hulks that came to land; but they themselves, meanwhile, were cast upon some shore yet further west, toward which we are all tending, and which we shall reach at last, it may be through storm and darkness, as they did.[6]

Thoreau then reflects on how the halcyon shores to which the dead emigrate remain invisible from Boston Harbor:

The mariner who makes the safest port in Heaven, perchance, seems to his friends on earth to be shipwrecked, for they deem Boston Harbor the better place; though perhaps invisible to them, a skillful pilot comes to meet him, and the fairest and balmiest gales blow off that coast, his good ship makes the land in halcyon days, and he kisses the shore in rapture there, while his old hulk tosses in the surf here. . . . If the *St. John* did not make her port here, she has been telegraphed there.[7]

Public and Private Talk about God

In *Walden*, Thoreau acknowledges a difference between his public and private views on the morality of fishing. "Whatever humanity I might conjure up against it," he confesses, "was factitious and concerned my philosophy more than my feelings." His speech about the divinity was similar. It changed with his mood, audience, and rhetorical purpose. When giving his philosophical opinion, or in his polemical riffs, he often sounds skeptical or cheekily defiant. Yet in his private poems, letters, and *Journal*, there is at times an affective, even touching, quality to his speech about, and occasionally to, God. He uses more conventional religious language and speaks more reverentially. "In the sunshine and the crowing of cocks I feel an illimitable holiness, which makes me bless God and myself," he wrote February 7, 1841. "I thank God for sorrow," he wrote in April 1842, a few months after John died. "Is not he kind still who lets this south wind blow, this warm sun shine on me?"[8]

On August 17, 1851, Thoreau walked in the woods in a low and desultory mood. Suddenly, his spirits were lifted by the sound of the wind in the trees, and he burst out in joy and gratitude, thanking God not in the third person, but in direct address:

> My heart leaps into my mouth at the sound of the wind
> in the woods. I, whose life was but yesterday so desultory
> and shallow, suddenly recover my spirits, my spirituality,
> through my hearing. . . . Now I have occasion to be grate-
> ful for the flood of life that is flowing over me. I am not
> so poor: I can smell the ripening apples; the very rills are
> deep; the autumnal flowers, the *Trichostema dichotomum*
> [forked bluecurls]—not only its bright blue flower above the
> sand, but its strong wormwood scent which belongs to the
> season—feed my spirit, endear the earth to me, make me
> value myself and rejoice; the quivering of pigeons' wings

reminds me of the tough fiber of the air which they rend. I thank you, God. . . . I do not deserve anything, I am unworthy of the least regard; and yet I am made to rejoice. I am impure and worthless, and yet the world is gilded for my delight.

Most of Thoreau's passionate entreaties or tender references to God occur in the late 1830s and early 1840s, and they begin well before John's death in January 1842, rather than as a response to it. In 1841, for example, Thoreau described sailing on Concord's rivers as being "blown on by God's breath," and he quoted Coleridge on the love of God. "We must securely love each other as we love God, with no more danger that our love be unrequited or ill-bestowed."[9]

Such familial or tender references decline in number in the 1850s, but they continue to appear in his private *Journal*. In October 1855, after recovering from five months of weakness in his legs that kept him mainly indoors, he wrote, "Methinks I am getting a little more strength into those knees of mine; and, for my part, I believe that God does delight in the strength of a man's legs." Two years after *Walden* came out, Thoreau thanked God for his life. "What you call bareness and poverty—is to me simplicity: God could not be unkind to me if he should try." And he described God as a mother on January 22, 1859. "As a mother loves to see her child imbibe nourishment and expand, so God loves to see his children thrive on the nutriment he has furnished them."[10]

The ever unpredictable Thoreau even spoke well, at least once, of traditional Christian speech, a prayer offered by a British explorer. In August 1852, he borrowed a copy of the recently published *Stray Leaves from an Arctic Journal*, Lieutenant Sherard Osborn's account of a Royal Navy expedition he led to the Arctic in 1850–51 to find the lost explorer John Franklin. Thoreau was struck by a prayer the British explorer offered before leaving England, which began:[11]

> O Lord God, our Heavenly Father, who teachest man knowledge, and givist him skill and power to accomplish his designs, we desire continually to wait, and call, and depend upon Thee. Thy way is in the sea, and Thy paths in the great waters. Thou rulest and commandest all things. We therefore draw nigh unto Thee for help in the great work which we now have to do.

Osborn then asks God for protection from physical harm and for "such strength and patience as may carry us through every toil and danger, whether by sea or land; and, if it be Thy good pleasure, vouchsafe to us a safe return to our families and homes."[12]

Rather than disdaining Osborn's prayer, as one might expect, Thoreau admired its direct address to God and the simple, humble trust it expressed. "I am struck by the ease and simplicity with which an Englishman expresses a sentiment of reverence for the author and ruler of the universe," he wrote. "It is very manly—and appears to some extent to characterize the nation. Osborn imprints with such simplicity a prayer prepared for the Arctic expedition."[13]

Naming God

There is a paradox in Thoreau's naming of God. In *A Week*, he disdained traditional speech about a personal God, calling it presumptuous to try to "fable the ineffable." However, he also portrayed God in figurative language, sometimes using the very anthropomorphic terms he criticized in the mouths of others. In his interior life, Thoreau sought to follow Emerson's advice to know God through direct, unmediated experience— and during such moments Thoreau said he was "powerless for expression." But in his vocation as a writer he needed the mediation of words and images in order to conceive of and express the divine. The actual interior experience is gold, Thoreau said, and the expression of it gold leaf.

> Though in the seasons when our genius reigns we may be powerless for expression, yet, in calmer seasons, when our talent is active, the memory of those rarer moods comes to color our picture and is the permanent paint-pot, as it were, into which we dip our brush. Thus no life or experience goes unreported at last; but if it be not solid gold it is gold-leaf, which gilds the furniture of the mind.[14]

As noted above, Thoreau used numerous figurative terms for God. While he did so mainly out of artistic and rhetorical necessity, it nevertheless underscores a difference between him and Emerson. One simply cannot imagine Thoreau's mentor using the names for God that Thoreau used. For Emerson, the natural world is largely a manifestation of pure ideality. His concept of divinity is largely of a god within. "In all my lectures, I have taught only one doctrine," Emerson wrote, "the infinitude of the private man." For him, according to Harold Bloom, God was "what was oldest and most original in oneself." In contrast, Thoreau's creative and personalized appellations convey a sense of a presence beyond himself, of a divine being as Other, which allows for the possibility of relationship. Such an implied relation is central to William James's definition of religion, which, as we saw in the introduction, is "the feelings, acts, and experiences" of individuals "so far as they apprehend themselves to *stand in relation* to whatever they may consider the divine [emphasis added]." In his *Varieties*, James also calls prayer "the very movement itself of the soul, putting itself in a personal relation of contact with the mysterious power of which it feels the presence—it may be even before it has a name by which to call it."[15]

Thoreau thus did not find it easy to follow Emerson's advice to "cleave to God against the name of God." His names for God were legion. He spoke (following the capitalization used in the Princeton editions) of the "Universal Soul," "the Unnamed," and "the Almighty" in *A Week* and "the All," "the Great spirit," and "divinity" in his *Journal*. He referred to a providential personal creator in *Walden*, using terms such as "Artist," "Builder," and "Benefactor"—and, in his *Journal*, "my maker," "the author and ruler of the universe," and "the great Master." He also used more playful terms, calling nature "the works of an old master" and referring to "a parable of the great teacher." In one poem, God is even the "Charioteer" who steers the planet. Thoreau also used slightly discordant or vaguely comic names for God, such as "the great chemist," "the Great Hare," "great Assessor," "Great Looker," and "Great Mower," as if in tacit acknowledgment that such metaphors are bound to fail.[16]

But even Thoreau drew the line. Although the liberal Unitarianism of his day was too lifeless and rational for him, he shared its aversion to the wrathful and arbitrary God of his Calvinist forebears. Thus one name for God he never used was *king*; nor did Thoreau ever ascribe to God the power or attributes of a Roman emperor. He used *lord* only in parody of conventional religious speech. His aversion to the portrait of God-as-punisher that can be found in the Bible is one the few things that remained consistent in Thoreau's religious thought. Another was his rejection of the divinity of Jesus.

By whatever name, or no name, the divine mystery Thoreau sought to commune with was beyond human efforts to corner or control it. But that did not make God indifferent to humanity, in Thoreau's view. Despite the challenge of portraying the divine, the experience of God's companionship was a key feature of Thoreau's theological thought.

ELEVEN

An Immortal Companion

In July 1845, as Thoreau was beginning his experiment at Walden, he briefly doubted if he could do without human society while living at the pond. His mood lifted, however, as he realized that the nearest companion to him was not a person in the village but the plant and animal life all around him.

> In the midst of a gentle rain while these thoughts prevailed, I was suddenly sensible of such sweet and beneficent society in Nature, in the very pattering of the drops, and in every sound and sight around my house, an infinite and unaccountable friendliness all at once like an atmosphere sustaining me, as made the fancied advantages of human neighborhood insignificant, and I have never thought of them since. Every little pine needle expanded and swelled with sympathy and befriended me.[1]

Such a view of pine needles might be viewed today as animism or what the biologist and naturalist E. O. Wilson has called "biophilia." More than a century ago, William James quoted that passage in *Walden* as an example of how the "presence of a higher and friendly Power" is a "fundamental feature in the spiritual life."[2]

In an undated journal entry around 1850, Thoreau admired the Hindus for having "perhaps a purer, more independent and impersonal knowledge of God" than "the Hebrews." Their scriptures offer an "inquisitive and contemplative access to God," not the "grosser and more personal repentance" of the Bible. Yet Thoreau, with his fondness for inconsistency and paradox, sometimes conveys a sense of having an intimate personal relation and even affection for a God whom he portrays as being close at hand. In *A Week*, he said whether you love Christ or Buddha does not matter because "the love is the main thing." I think he meant that. "My love is invulnerable," he wrote in late 1841. "Meet me on that ground, and you will find me strong. When I am condemned, and condemn myself utterly, I think straightway, but I rely on my love for some things. Therein I am whole and entire. Therein I am God-propt [propped]."[3]

Thoreau was fond of Chaucer and praised the down-to-earth medieval English poet's sense of familiarity with and affection for God. "Chaucer's familiar, but innocent, way of speaking of God is of a piece with his character. He comes readily to his thoughts without any false reverence. . . . God should come into our thoughts with no more parade than the zephyr [breeze] into our ears. Only strangers approach him with ceremony. How rarely in our English tongue do we find expressed any affection for God. No sentiment is so rare as love of God."[4]

Formal religion lacked that tender feeling for Thoreau. "The protestant church seems to have nothing to supply the place of the Saints of the catholic calendar, who were at least channels for the affections," he wrote. "Its [the Protestant] God has perhaps too many of the attributes of a Scandinavian deity."[5]

Instead of the foreboding and distant deity of his childhood swooping down from on high as a judge, the God Thoreau knew was close at hand, woven into every twig, trunk, and blade. Nature's very motions were the circulations of God. "The flowing sail, the running stream, the waving tree, the roving wind—whence else their infinite health and freedom? I can see nothing so holy as unrelaxed play and frolic in this bower God has built for us. The suspicion of sin never comes to this thought. Oh, if men felt this way they would never build temples even of marble or diamond" but would "disport" forever in this paradise.[6]

What Others Get by Churchgoing

The closeness Thoreau felt to the divine was inseparable from the warmth he felt toward the natural world, which he described as being "of a religious or else love-cracked character." And it could not be understood in the abstract. A person must be aware of a "certain friendliness" in nature and have a nearly personal relationship with it, he said. "I cannot conceive of any life which deserves the name, unless there is a certain tender relation to nature. This it is which makes winter warm, and supplies society in the desert and wilderness." Just such society was supplied to Thoreau on a bleak winter day in January 1857. Out alone in the woods, he suddenly had a feeling of being "grandly related" to all things in nature. He then imagined the presence of an invisible, immortal companion—his awareness of which filled him with "what others get by churchgoing."[7]

In the street and in society I am almost invariably cheap
and dissipated, my life is unspeakably mean. . . . But alone
in distant woods or fields, in unpretending sprout lands or
pastures tracked by rabbits, even on a black and, to most,
cheerless day, like this, when a villager would be thinking
of his inn, I come to myself. I once more feel myself grandly
related, and that the cold and solitude are friends of mine.
I suppose that this value, in my case, is equivalent to what
others get by churchgoing and prayer . . . It is as if I always
met in those places some grand, serene, immortal, infinitely
encouraging, though invisible, companion, and walked
with him.[8]

Thoreau's desire for or feeling of having such a companion is telling. Such an imagined presence helps him "come
to [him]self," or be more fully alive. In *Walden*, Thoreau describes another imagined encounter with a godlike presence,
whom he calls "the old settler and original proprietor of
Walden Pond." Thoreau is certainly being droll in the passage,
and having fun doing so, but the fact that he imagines God as
a jovial acquaintance with whom he spends pleasant hours is
significant to his theological thought. It shows how much he
values having an original relation with creation.

I have occasional visits in the long winter evenings, when
the snow falls fast and the wind howls in the wood, from an
old settler and original proprietor, who is reported to have
dug Walden Pond, and stoned it, and fringed it with pine
woods; who tells me stories of old time and of new eternity;
and between us we manage to pass a cheerful evening with
social mirth and pleasant views of things, even without
apples or cider—a most wise and humorous friend, whom I
love much.

And though "he is thought to be dead," none can show where he is buried, Thoreau adds, reminding us, incidentally, that the "God is dead" movement has been around a long time.⁹

Thoreau's notion of God incorporated such paradoxical elements. It is at once "wild above all," possessing a strange, awesome otherness, and also a kind, encouraging, familiar presence. As if to balance his description of the patriarchal old settler, Thoreau speaks in the same paragraph of an even more natural creative force—a "ruddy and lusty old dame" who dwells in his "neighborhood," in whose Edenic herb garden he loves to stroll. The old dame delights in all seasons, has an unequaled genius for fertility, and her memory runs back further than myth. In *Walden*, Thoreau creates a male god and then a female fertility one.¹⁰

After describing the ruddy dame, Thoreau expresses his affinity with the earth. "Shall I not have intelligence with the earth?" he asks. "Am I not partly leaves and vegetable mould myself?" The next line in the first version of the manuscript, which Thoreau began in 1846, was, "God is my father & my friend—men are my brothers—but nature is my mother & my sister." Thoreau struck that line in his next draft (he may have thought it sounded too traditional) but the sentiment accords with the sense of intimacy with God he periodically voiced in his *Journal*.¹¹

Thoreau was consistent throughout his life that God was to be met without fear or formality. "When you travel to the Celestial City, carry no letter of introduction," he wrote Harrison Blake in 1848. "When you knock, ask to see God—none of the servants." Eleven years later, he saw no need for ceremony in approaching God. "Men of science," he wrote March 8, 1859, "when they pause to mention 'the power, wisdom, and goodness' of God, or, as they sometimes call him, 'the Almighty Designer,' speak of him as a total stranger whom it is necessary to treat with the highest consideration. They seem suddenly to have lost their wits."[12]

A Natural Gift of Grace

Thoreau experienced the divinity of the natural world as a source of redemption from a shallow, misguided, or trivial life, and he believed that God bestows this gift on all persons, regardless of merit. One does not need to believe anything to be saved by wildness; one has only to purify one's senses and awaken to the infinite gift continuously being poured out around us. Redemption is a matter of seeing things aright. On January 26, 1852, he quoted a remark by Daniel Foster, the staunchly antislavery pastor of Concord's Trinitarian Church, whom he respected. "I hear of one good thing Foster said in his sermon the other day, the subject being Nature: 'Thank God, there is no doctrine of election with regard to Nature! We are all admitted to her.'" The term *election* refers to the Puritan "covenant of grace," the belief that God freely "elects" or bestows salvation on certain individuals, called the elect, and gives them the grace needed to persevere in their faith. Thoreau's view of nature was similar to the Puritan view of grace. This is a main theme of *Walden*, in which Thoreau styles himself the beneficiary of such grace. "As I walked on the railroad causeway, I used to wonder at the halo of light around my shadow, and would fain fancy myself one of the elect."[13]

Thoreau sometimes felt unworthy to receive such divine favor. "Notwithstanding that I regard myself as a good deal of a scamp, yet for the most part the spirit of the universe is unaccountably kind to me, and I enjoy perhaps an unusual share of happiness," he wrote in his *Journal* for 1850. (True to his Puritan roots, he added, "Yet I question sometimes if there is not some settlement to come.") A week after mov-

ing to Walden, he described himself in his *Journal* as inex-
plicably guided by the divine. "Sometimes when I compare
myself with other men, methinks I am favored by the Gods.
They seem to whisper joy to me beyond my deserts and that
I do have a solid warrant and surety at their hands, which my
fellows do not. . . . I am especially guided and guarded."[14]

Thoreau's sense of having a personal relation with God
likely had more than theological roots. Despite the sensitivity of his soul and his evident desire for love, Thoreau had
few channels for affection in his life outside his family. His
personality—in particular, his dismissal of common social
graces as superficial—struck people as insular and off putting. Emerson dwelled somewhat oddly on this aspect of
Thoreau in his funeral eulogy, although he may have been
rationalizing the failure of their friendship, consciously or
otherwise. He called Thoreau's tendency to be oppositional "a
little chilling to the social affections." Even toward his admir-
ers, Thoreau "was never affectionate, but superior, didactic—
scorning their petty ways."[15]

Thoreau nevertheless placed a high value on friendship
and especially on the grand Platonic *ideal* of love or friendship, which was close to the religious sentiment for Thoreau.
"In friendship," he wrote in his *Journal*, "we worship moral
beauty without the formality of religion." He believed that because true friends would silently know each other's thoughts,
any words actually spoken between them were more likely to
sully, rather than deepen, their bond. Thoreau's family and a
few friends, including Ellery Channing and Bronson Alcott,
were intensely loyal to him, but generally, his personality
and his high standards for friendship both worked against his
having actual intimacy with others. Emerson said so bluntly
in his eulogy. "I think the severity of his ideal interfered to
deprive him of a healthy sufficiency of human society."[16]

Thoreau acknowledged being drawn toward certain persons only to be disappointed. "I love my friends very much, but I find that it is of no use to go to see them," he wrote on November 16, 1850. "I hate them commonly when I am near them. They belie themselves and deny me continually." Thoreau's thin skin did not help. If he heard that a friend spoke of him with merely a "cold and indifferent tone," he was deeply offended. "What treachery I feel it to be! The sum of all crimes against humanity!" Such sensitivity and unrealistic standards did not bode well for his relationships. "If I have not succeeded in my friendships," he admitted, "it was because I demanded more of them and did not put up with what I could get." Yet Thoreau's numerous reflections on love, and his anguished brooding in his *Journal* over the loss of his intimacy with Emerson, make clear that he deeply desired such intimacy.[17]

Thoreau's sense of God as a familiar and friendly presence was real, but there may have been a degree to which he substituted divine love for human love. "Between whom there is hearty truth, there is love; and in proportion to our truthfulness and confidence in one another, our lives are divine and miraculous," he wrote in *A Week*. Such ties "anticipate Heaven for us." Perhaps the reverse was true for Thoreau, and his affection for God "anticipated" the human friendship he pined for yet drove away.[18]

A Telegram from Heaven

After the telegraph came to Concord in the 1840s, Thoreau repeatedly delighted in listening to the tonal vibrations in the wooden poles caused by the wind passing through the wires, and he wrote about it often. One day in 1851, Thoreau he felt that the wires were conveying a personal message from heaven to him, which he emphasized in his *Journal* by using

dialogue. The mystical voice urged him to persevere and as-
sured him that there is a yet higher plane of life.

> It told me by the faintest imaginable strain, it told me by the
> finest strain that a human ear can hear, yet conclusively and
> past all refutation, that there were higher, infinitely higher,
> planes of life which it behooved me never to forget. As I
> was entering the Deep Cut, the wind, which was conveying
> a message to me from heaven, dropped it on the wire of the
> telegraph which it vibrated as it passed. I instantly sat down
> on a stone at the foot of the telegraph-pole, and attended to
> the communication. It said: "Bear in mind, Child, and never
> for an instant forget, that there are higher planes, infinitely
> higher planes, of life than this thou art now traveling on.
> Know that the goal is distant, and is upward, and is worthy
> all your life's efforts to attain to." And then it ceased, and
> though I sat some minutes longer I heard nothing more.[19]

It is hard to know how seriously to take Thoreau's intimate
portrayals of God. But his use of the phrase "Bear in mind,
Child" speaks to the tender, personal terms that he at least
sometimes saw himself on with heaven.

TWELVE

Thoreau and the "Prince of Radicals"

Thoreau's borrowings from Christian frameworks raise the question of whether he could by any stretch be called Christian. It does not appear that he could. In all his references to religion, both personal and critical, one important figure in Western religion whom Thoreau all but ignores is Jesus. The Christian term *Jesus Christ* appears once in *Walden*, and in his *Journal* of nearly two million words it appears once in his own voice and once in quotation. The name Jesus, by itself, does not appear in the *Journal*. Thoreau does refer to *Christ* several times, but always as a literary, historical, or political reference to the central figure of the Gospels, and usually as a rhetorical foil in his social criticism rather than as an expression of faith in Jesus as *the* Christ, the son of God, or Messiah. The catkins of the willow were the only redeemers Thoreau accepted. He was not big on monuments, and the church's elaborate theological conception of Christ was for him a bronze statue that the world could do without. His dismissal of the divinity of Jesus is a constant feature of his religious thought.

Thoreau's reported deathbed quip to an old friend who

was concerned about the state of his soul that "a snowstorm meant more to him than Christ" conceals a more complicated relationship, however. Like other Transcendentalists in his day, Thoreau had a push-pull relationship with Jesus, alternately admiring and demoting him, sometimes in the same sentence. While Thoreau did not worship Jesus, he revered his social justice teachings, saying, "It is not necessary to be Christian to appreciate the beauty and significance of the life of Christ."

Thoreau quoted the New Testament often and used it as a literary cudgel in his polemics against the church and in his critique of the moral quagmire in America. "If Christ should appear on earth," he wrote three days after the abolitionist John Brown was arrested for insurrection, "he would on all hands be denounced as a mistaken, misguided man, insane and crazed." The humanity, voluntary poverty, practical morality, and radicalness of Jesus appealed to Thoreau. He had contempt for the "respectable Christianity" of his day, but it is not hard to imagine that, had Thoreau lived in the second century, before the elevation of the doctrine of the trinity, he might have been among the catacomb Christians persecuted by Rome.[1]

Jesus and the Fugitive

Thoreau's single use of *Jesus Christ* in his *Journal* illustrates the appeal the Christian ethos held for him. In April 1851, Thomas Sims, an enslaved man from Georgia who had escaped north, was captured in Boston under the new Fugitive Slave Act and returned to his enslaver. The most controversial part of the "Compromise of 1850," the odious new law compelled people in Free States to assist in returning escaped slaves. Although intended to defuse the growing tension between North and South, the law actually contributed to the rupture between them. Thoreau was incensed that "a perfectly innocent man" was marched down to a Boston pier in chains by armed policemen, forced onto a ship, and sent back "into a slavery as complete as the world ever knew." Paraphrasing Jesus's words in Matthew 25:40 to care for the most vulnerable, Thoreau speculated that the Nazarene rebel would have taken Sims's place in order to let him remain free.

> Of course it makes not the least difference—I wish you to consider this—who the man was, whether he was Jesus Christ or another, for inasmuch as ye did it unto the least of these his brethren ye did it unto him. Do you think *he* would have stayed here in *liberty* and let the black man go into slavery in his stead?[2]

In 1854, the case of Anthony Burns, another fugitive African forcibly returned to his enslavers in the South, drew rare praise from Thoreau for Christians as a group—because the ethics of their scripture compelled them to oppose the return of Burns. Here he compares Burns to the figure of Christ and implicitly likens the Massachusetts judge who decided Burns's fate to Pontius Pilate.

> While they are hurrying off Christ to the cross, the ruler decides he cannot *constitutionally* interfere to save him. The Christians, now and always, are they who obey the higher law, who discover it to be according to their constitution to interfere. They at least cut off the ears of the police; the others pocket the thirty pieces of silver. This was meaner than to crucify Christ, for he could better take care of himself.[3]

Thoreau also referred to Jesus positively in *A Week*. "Christ," he wrote, is a "sublime actor on the stage of the world" and "the prince of Reformers and Radicals." High praise—but the reference to reformers and radicals suggests that one of Thoreau's motives in lauding Jesus was to chastise Christianity for failing to live up to his ideals. Thoreau even used Jesus as a foil against his beloved ancient Hindus, whom he presented as being so absorbed in Brahma, the Hindu god of creation, and so inward and withdrawn, as to be morally passive and "stagnant." In Thoreau's alternative Christian cosmology, the "youth" from Bethlehem, with his practical concern for the poor, brings Brahma "down to earth and to mankind" as a new avatar or reincarnation of Brahma.[4]

So many years and ages of the gods those Eastern sages sat contemplating Brahm, uttering in silence the mystic 'Om,' being absorbed into the essence of the Supreme Being, never going out of themselves, but subsiding farther and deeper within; so infinitely wise, yet infinitely stagnant; until, at last, in that same Asia, but in the western part of it, appeared a youth, wholly unforetold by them—not being absorbed into Brahm, but bringing Brahm down to earth and to mankind; in whom Brahm had awaked from his long sleep, and exerted himself, and the day began—a new avatar. The Brahman had never thought to be a brother of mankind as well as a child of God.[5]

Thoreau also conveyed his regard for Jesus in a letter to Blake in 1850. He would be sorry, Thoreau wrote, if he had lived in the golden age of Greece and "visited Olympus even, but fell asleep after dinner, and did not hear the conversation of the Gods" or if he had "lived in Judea eighteen hundred

able Christianity' that is at all generally embraced in the two countries."[10]

Thoreau was also scornful of how the church cited Christ's teachings, as it interpreted them, to enforce conformity of thought and hammer home its authority. "There was a man who lived a long, long time ago, and his name was Moses, and another whose name was Christ, and if your thought does not, or does not appear to, coincide with what they said, [people] have no ears to hear you."[11]

The Sermon on Fair Haven Hill

Thoreau was nevertheless drawn by the New Testament, or at least by the first three overlapping narratives known as the synoptic Gospels (he shows little regard for the more esoteric Gospel of John) and quoted from the New Testament extensively. It is "remarkable for its pure morality," its lessons come naturally "to the lips of all Protestants," and it provides "the most pregnant and practical texts," Thoreau wrote in *A Week*. Its pragmatism was among its chief appeals. "There is no harmless dreaming, no wise speculation in it, but everywhere a substratum of good sense. . . . There is no poetry in it, we may say, nothing regarded in the light of beauty merely, but moral truth is its object. All mortals are convicted by its conscience."[12]

But apparently not all mortals. Thoreau complained several times about the Gospels' lack of traction in his society. He implied that the New Testament is little read when he said, with mock seriousness, that he could not find anyone to talk to about it. He wanted to read it aloud to his friends, he claimed, because it "fit their case exactly," and he was sure they had never heard of it. When he tried, however, they soon showed that "it is wearisome to them," and he despaired of getting their ears. Thoreau admitted it was a hard book to put into practice himself. "I love this book rarely, though it is a sort of castle in the air to me, which I am permitted to dream."[13]

Nevertheless, he continued to defend it—and his own love of it. In 1852, Thoreau recalled how Horace Greeley, in his review of *A Week* three years earlier, had criticized him for speaking of the New Testament in his own words and thoughts. "The one thought I had" upon reading that, Thoreau wrote, "was that it would give me real pleasure to know that he loved it as sincerely and enlightenedly as I did; but I felt that he did not care so much about it as I."[14]

Crucifying John Brown

Thoreau's tone about Jesus becomes more radical after John Brown's failed raid on the federal armory at Harpers Ferry in October 1859. Thoreau was an ardent admirer of the uncompromising abolitionist, who was hung for insurrection on December 2, and he devoted much of his *Journal* in fall 1859 to him, pouring out 6,500 words about Brown on October 22 alone. For Thoreau, the castle in the air now had a foundation he could defend and praise.

Thoreau valorized Brown by linking his fate to the crucifixion of Jesus. "A government that pretends to be Christian and crucifies a million Christs every day!" he exclaimed on October 13—a line Thoreau would work into his impassioned Concord speech and essay "A Plea for John Brown." And the same day: "A church that can never have done with excommunicating Christ while it exists."[15]

"Some eighteen hundred years ago," Thoreau wrote in his *Journal* a week later, "Christ was crucified; this morning, perhaps, John Brown was hung. These are the two ends of a chain which I rejoice to know is not without its links." On October 22, Thoreau again compared Brown to Christ. "You," he railed at Brown's persecutors, "who pretend to care for Christ crucified, consider what you are about to do to him who offered himself to be the savior of four millions of men!"[16]

Finally, three days after Brown was hung, Thoreau conferred a kind of divinity on him, declaring Brown immortal. He pretended to not understand how Brown could have been killed—the idea he represented being so deathless—and hinted at Brown's resurrection by invoking his "translation" to "pure spirit."

> On the day of his translation, I heard, to be sure, that he was hung, but I did not know what that meant, and I felt no sorrow on his account; but not for a day or two did I even hear that he was dead, and not after any number of days shall I believe it. Of all the men who are said to be my contemporaries, it seems to me that John Brown is the only one who has not died. I meet him at every turn. He is more alive than ever he was. He is not confined to North Elba nor to Kansas. He is no longer working in secret only. John Brown has earned immortality.[17]

Even among Thoreau's contemporaries who recognized his deep spirituality, few, understandably, thought of Thoreau as Christian. Louisa May Alcott dissented. She described Thoreau as a "real" Christian, at least in deed. At his funeral on May 9, 1862, her father, Bronson Alcott, read from Thoreau's writings. His words were not then considered appropriate for a church service, which, Louisa speculated, may be why Bronson read them. "Father read selections from Henry's own books, for many people said he was an infidel and as he never went to church when living, he ought not to be carried there dead," Louisa wrote to an admirer of Thoreau two days after the funeral. "If ever a man was a real Christian it was Henry, and I think his own wise and pious thoughts read by one who loved him, and whose own life was a beautiful example of religious faith, convinced many and touched the hearts of all."[18]

THIRTEEN

An Inkwell in Heaven

Another clue to the puzzle of Thoreau's religion is his extensive and often subversive use of religious language. Thoreau draped nature in religious terms and phrases to convey its sanctity. He also sought to take such language back from its institutional custodians and reframe its meaning for his readers. Who else but Thoreau could say, as he does in "Wild Fruits," that, come the fall harvest, nature places both communion table and altar before us. "We pluck and eat in remembrance of her. It is a sort of sacrament—a Communion—the not forbidden fruits, which no serpent tempts us to eat."[1]

Scholars who have mined all of Thoreau's writings for direct or indirect references to the Bible have cited some five hundred allusions. It is true that many of these references, including "new wine in old bottles," "the apple of his eye," "swaddling clothes," "the birds of the air," or a lifespan being "threescore years and ten" have long since passed into everyday English. Others are only tenuously linked to a biblical passage. By the standards of the birds and flowers, Thoreau says, he expects his life to "have been found wanting." This may refer to the Daniel 5:27, "Thou art weighed in the balances, and art found wanting," but to me the evidence is not persuasive. However, Thoreau's famous declaration in *The Maine Woods* that the pine tree is as immortal as he is and will perchance "go to as high a heaven" bears more than a passing similarity to Job's declaration, in Job 11:8, that God's will is impossible to know. "It is as high as heaven: what canst thou do? Deeper than hell: what canst thou know?" It is safe to say there are hundreds of such allusions.[2]

Thoreau loved the Bible, which he called "the Book of Books," for its grounding in the natural world, its artistry, and its earnest, earthy prose. He learned it at home and in "Sabbath School" at First Parish, which began formally in 1818, the year after he was born. One of the books taught in it was *The Bible Class Text Book; or Biblical Catechism Containing Questions Historical, Doctrinal, Practical and Experimental, Designed to Promote an Intimate Acquaintance with the Inspired Volume,* by Hervey Wilbur, published in 1823 by Cummings & Hillard in Boston. Thoreau had nothing good to say about schools in general, let alone one run by a church, and it is hard to imagine that he did not squirm until being sprung out of doors. But Sabbath school gave Thoreau the beginnings of an acquaintance with the Bible that would deepen and serve as a key element in his unique literary style.[3]

Biblical Wine in New Bottles

Thoreau turned to the Bible to express his ideas about justice, time, the futility of materialism, and the true purpose of life. "By a seeming fate, commonly called necessity," he writes in *Walden,* alluding to Matthew 6:19–21, people "are employed, as it says in an old book, laying up treasures which moth and rust will corrupt and thieves break through and steal." However, he did not view the Bible as the unerring revelation of God. He once criticized English philosopher and art critic John Ruskin for accepting the Bible too literally. "The love of Nature and fullest perception of the revelation which she is to man is not compatible with the belief in the peculiar revelation of the Bible" that Ruskin expressed, Thoreau wrote. Thoreau was also critical of what he saw as of the severity and arbitrary administration of divine justice in the Bible.[4]

Thoreau rendered his daily life in religious terms. "I find that I conciliate the gods by some sacrament as bathing, or abstemiousness in diet, or rising early, and directly they smile on me," he wrote in 1849. "These are my sacraments." He used religious language in order to vest his views with cultural and literary authority. At his Harvard commencement in 1837, he dressed his radical critique of America's growing commercial ethos, with its emphasis on work as an end in itself, in the language of the Sabbath. People spend too much time performing work to support their consumption, he thought. Rather than working six days and resting one, he proposed, people should labor one day a week and reserve the other six for a "Sabbath of the affections and the soul."[5]

Thoreau also looked at the question of how we should get a living through a religious lens in the lecture that grew out of his Walden experience, "Life without Principle." His most frequently given lecture, it was initially titled "What Shall It Profit"—an allusion to Mark 8:36 (KJV): "For what shall it profit a man, if he shall gain the whole world, and lose his own soul?" The lecture is the closest thing to a sermon that Thoreau gave. It criticizes the secularizing effect of industrial capitalism, declaring the world to be an "infinite bustle" of work and business in which "there is no sabbath." The rush to find gold is blasphemous, Thoreau argues, because it turns God into a "moneyed gentleman" who scatters pennies in order to see people scramble for them. He also warns in the lecture against trivial news, gossip, and mindless entertainment, which he calls a grave peril to the soul. If we have "desecrated ourselves" by yielding to such distractions, Thoreau says, "the remedy will be by wariness and devotion to reconsecrate ourselves, and make once more a fane [temple] of the mind." Bradley P. Dean, who reconstructed the essay's evolution over eight years, has identified sixteen biblical allusions in it.[6]

Thoreau continued to use religious language in his later *Journal*, if less often. In 1857, he felt that a melody he heard connected him to the farthest reaches of the universe. With music, "we attain to a wisdom that passeth understanding," he wrote, paraphrasing Jesus. On the river that fall, he hauled home a large, white oak log to cut up and burn that winter. Green moss still adhered to the waterlogged wood. "These old stumps stand like anchorites [religious recluses] and yogees," he wrote, "putting off their earthly garments, more and more sublimed from year to year, ready to be translated, and then they are ripe for my fire. I administer the last sacrament and purification."[7]

In his late essay "Autumnal Tints," the fall leaves contentedly "return to dust again and are laid low, resigned to lie and decay at the foot of the tree." The line echoes the fate of Adam, as told by God, in Genesis 3:19: "For dust thou art, and unto dust shalt return." In traditional Christian typography, "the tree" is also a cipher for the cross of crucifixion.[8]

In October 1860, he was delighted to find lilies in a new artificial pond in Sleepy Hollow Cemetery. Thoreau had laid out the pond's location in his survey of the site five years earlier. "In this pond thus dug in the midst of a meadow a year or two ago and supplied by springs in the meadow, I find today several small patches of the large yellow and the kalmiana lily already established. Thus in the midst of death we are in life." Again Thoreau flips a religious quotation to serve his purpose. "In the midst of life we are in death" appears in the prayer for the burial of the dead in the 1662 Book of Common Prayer.[9]

The Westminster Shorter Catechism adopted by the Puritans in 1647 was a favorite foil. As a boy, Thoreau had to learn its first lesson, that the chief end of man is to "glorify God and enjoy him forever." In his writings, he suggests that the way to do that is to glorify and enjoy nature. In 1852 he called the first treatise on forestry, John Evelyn's *Sylva*, published in 1664, "a new kind of prayer-book, a glorifying of the trees and enjoying them forever, which was the chief end of his life." A year later, he wondered if anyone had noticed a particularly beautiful day. "Will the haymaker when he comes home tonight know that this has been such a beautiful day? It is like a great and beautiful flower unnamed. Is not such a day worthy of a hymn? It is such a day as mankind might spend in praising and glorifying nature." In 1854, he wrote that crickets were fulfilling the catechism's view of the chief end of life with their chant. "It is no transient love strain, hushed when the incubating season is past, but a glorifying of God and enjoying of him forever." In 1859, he blasted the state of Massachusetts for noticing insects only to the extent that they were noxious to farming. "The catechism says that the chief end of man is to glorify God and enjoy him forever, which of course is applicable mainly to God as seen in his works. Yet the only account of its beautiful insects butterflies, etc. which God has made and set before us which the State ever thinks of spending any money on is the account of those which are injurious to vegetation! . . . This is the way we glorify God and enjoy him forever."[10]

Longing to Go on Pilgrimage

Even Thoreau's more secular writing often has a subtle but pervasive religious character that is easy to overlook or dismiss as mere ornament. In his great intellectual biography of Thoreau, Robert D. Richardson calls Thoreau's "Walking" "a pointedly secular essay," a view shared by many. The essay's emphasis of the centrality of nature to human life and the salvific power of wildness tends to obscure its references to religion, but it is marked throughout by religious idioms. It begins by casting walking as a pilgrimage—a crusade, even— into a new kind of Holy Land, the heart of nature. The crow of a barnyard cock is the soundest philosophy, Thoreau writes, and a more recent and relevant one to our lives than an ancient text. "It is a newer testament—the Gospel according to the present moment."[11]

Thoreau's rooster has gotten up early and is fully awake. His crow is a burst of health, "a new fountain of the muses." So pure it is, "who has not betrayed his master many times since last he heard that note"—a reference to Jesus predicting that Peter would betray him three times before next crow of the cock.[12]

The walk we take through the woods, or on a country road, Thoreau writes, "is perfectly symbolical of the path we love to travel in the interior and ideal world." The sanity required and the desire to undertake it, however, "comes only by the grace of God. It requires a direct dispensation from heaven to become a walker."[13]

Most of us are too often like the worldly miser he describes in "Walking" who went to find his property bounds with his surveyor. Although it was actually heaven where the miser stood, he did not see the angels around him "but was looking for an old post-hole in the midst of paradise." Thoreau then imagines seeing the miser standing in the middle a boggy fen surrounded by devils. The man finds his bounds—"three little stones where a stake had been driven, and looking nearer I saw that the Prince of Darkness was his surveyor."[14]

Rather than lifting up the Bible, Thoreau often turns it upside down in "Walking." Comparing the American wilderness to the Garden of Eden, he writes that "Adam in paradise is not more favorably situated than the backwoodsman in this country. It is too late to be studying Hebrew; it is more important to understand even the slang today." But it is not too late to rewrite sacred verse. "I believe in the forest, and in the meadow, and in the night in which the corn grows," Thoreau declares, echoing the structure and syntax of the Apostles' Creed ("I believe in God the Father . . ."). Richardson and Alan Hodder both hear mockery in Thoreau's line. I hear a note of emulation and a poet's creative ear as he uses the old to write his newer testament.[15]

Thoreau's essay presents walking as a retreat to a sacred place and a means of self-renewal. "When I would recreate myself, I seek the darkest wood, the thickest and most interminable, and, to a citizen, most dismal swamp. I enter a swamp as a sacred place—a *sanctum sanctorum*," or holy of holies. "There is the strength—the marrow of Nature."[16]

Thoreau returns to his pilgrimage theme in "Walking" by quoting from the prologue to *The Canterbury Tales*. In it, Chaucer introduces the "palmers" (palm-bearing pilgrims), who "longen," or desire, more distant and holier strands or stretches of land than they know at home:

Than longen folk to go on pilgrimages,
And palmers for to seken strange strondes.[17]

For Thoreau, Chaucer's pilgrims are walking in the spirit of his essay. "So we saunter toward the Holy Land," he concludes, "till one day the sun shall shine more brightly than ever he has done, shall perchance shine into our minds and hearts, and light up our whole lives with a great awakening light, so warm and serene and golden as on a bank side in Autumn."[18]

In the introduction to this book, I recalled Thoreau's pretense of confusion over how to interpret the ban that a lyceum put on the topic of religion. He said he did not know what religion meant to his hosts, so he went ahead and told "of what religion I have experienced." The audience, he said, never knew he had come close to the topic. Thoreau wrote those words in December 1856, the morning after speaking to the lyceum in Amherst, New Hampshire, which was located in the Congregational church. (Having spoken in its basement, he said he hoped his talk had undermined its foundation.) The lecture in which he told of his religious experience was his "secular" essay "Walking."[19]

The Choicest of Relics

It is not surprising that Thoreau's work is suffused with Christian poetics. Protestant Christianity is largely a religion of the book. The Reformation shifted the focus of faith from sacrament and ritual to scripture and sermon. Although Thoreau was a naturalist, philosopher, and social critic, he was, above all, a writer. A word, he said, is a choicer relic than a stone from Chartres or Thebes. The word use, rhythm, and phraseology of the Bible had a profound influence on him. Thoreau pretended at times to know Eastern scriptures better, but as Walter Harding has noted, his "familiarity with the King James Bible is obvious on almost every page he wrote."[20]

Thoreau used the Bible selectively. In addition to dismissing its divine origin, he disdained its violence and its deference to received wisdom and tradition. Yet it is hard to imagine that Thoreau would have worked so diligently and so often with the literary form and content of a book he did not respect and find meaningful. A nonreligious writer would not have crafted a style employing it regularly, as illustrated by the relative lack of biblical allusion in such contemporaries as Cooper, Poe, Alcott, or Whitman. Even Emerson, Hawthorne, and Melville, whose writings are richly infused by a sense of religion, use explicit biblical and religious terms less often than does Thoreau. Thoreau uses them for stylistic purposes, but they are also more than literary devices. They enable Thoreau to offer a fundamentally religious vision of our relationship with nature.

FOURTEEN

"Go Thou My Incense"

Thoreau plays with religious language repeatedly and masterfully in *Walden*, his spiritual summons to an examined life, which he began at the pond but the bulk of which he wrote in the early 1850s. He invokes terms and idioms from the Bible and his Puritan heritage and recasts their meaning at every turn. Heaven is not only over our heads and under our feet in his masterpiece—it is everywhere. Some form of the word *heaven*, as a symbol of life lived in accord with nature and its divine source, appears four dozen times in the book.

Walden has been viewed by many interpreters as a sacred text about our relation to the "higher law." The Harvard philosopher Stanley Cavell, whose work is principally secular, has called it a "scripture" with its own parables, prophecies, hymns, and epics. He also sees Thoreau seeking to both "overturn" and revise Christianity as "his way of continuing it." Walter Harding, the primary founder of the Thoreau Society in 1941, has called it "a guide to the higher life" that "reaches its highest levels as a spiritual autobiography," saying it is "as much a religious document as any scripture." And Joyce Carol

Oates wrote of reading *Walden*: "I discovered Thoreau at the age of fifteen and found him the very voice of my inarticulate soul."[1]

About a third of the religious references in *Walden* are to Asian and other non-Christian belief systems—chiefly, Hindu and Confucian thought, with a few nods at Persian and Greek religion. Each morning, Thoreau writes, "I bathe my intellect in the stupendous and cosmogonal philosophy" of the Bhagavad Gita. He imagines that as he goes to his well for water, he meets "the servant of the Brahmin, priest of Brahma and Vishnu and Indira," who is drawing water for his master, that they grate buckets, and the "pure Walden water is mingled with the sacred water of the Ganges." And he lampoons the hired evangelical farmworker who believes "his second birth and peculiar religious experience" to be singular and exclusive in nature, whereas "Zoroaster, thousands of years ago, traveled the same road and had the same experience; but he, being wise, knew it to be universal."[2]

Thoreau mainly chose, however, to express his religious vision in *Walden* in the lingua franca of his Protestant culture, the Bible. Dozens of different versions of the Bible did not compete for popular use as they do today. The authoritative King James Version (KJV) was the standard, and it offered a rich fount of verbal imagery and resonant phraseology for Thoreau to alchemize with his genius. Biblical language flows like a coded stream through *Walden*, not only in specific words but also in Thoreau's reworking of biblical rhythms and cadences. "Walden was dead and is alive again" paraphrases Luke 15:24 ("This son of mine was dead and is alive again; he was lost and is found!")[3]

Walden is exceptional among Thoreau's works for its use of biblical language. In a single sentence about Indians who showed bravery and equanimity even as they were burned at the stake by missionaries, he manages to allude to the golden rule enjoined in Luke 6:31 ("as ye would that men should do to you"), Matthew 5:44 ("love your enemies") and Luke 23:34 ("forgive them; for they know not what they do").

> Being superior to physical suffering, it sometimes chanced that they [the Native Americans] were superior to any consolation which the missionaries could offer; and the law to do as you would be done by fell with less persuasiveness on the ears of those who, for their part, did not care how they were done by, who loved their enemies after a new fashion, and came very near freely forgiving them all they did.[4]

Thoreau refers in *Walden* to "manna" (the food God provided the Israelites) and removing the "motes" from one's eye (Luke 6:41–42). He sees no one in Concord "eating locusts and wild honey," like John the Baptist, and he complains that the inequities of "civilized" life are accepted too easily. "What mean ye by saying that the poor ye have always with you [Matthew 26:11] or that the fathers have eaten sour grapes, and the children's teeth are set on edge [Ezekiel 18:2]?" At least sixty-nine direct allusions have been matched to chapter and verse in the Bible: thirty-three to the Hebrew Bible and thirty-six to the New Testament. Twenty-one—almost two-thirds of the latter—are to the Gospel of Matthew, which contains the Sermon on the Mount and emphasizes Jesus's radical social justice teachings.[5]

A Charmed Circle

In 1851, Thoreau felt "inexpressibly begrimed" when, as a surveyor, he walked Concord's town line with coarse, "mean and narrow-minded" men representing the abutting towns. He later faulted himself for not protecting the "charmed circle which I have drawn around my abode" (that is, his spiritual life). Thoreau drew such a circle around his abode at Walden. That was why he went there in July 1845—to create a sacred domain centered around the pond. He signaled his religious aim in his *Journal* that first summer. "Verily a good house is a temple," he wrote three days after moving in, one "fit to entertain a traveling god," a place "where a goddess might trail her garments." His house, as he describes it in *Walden*, is less a shelter than a crystallization in white pine around his soul. The lake next to him is "earth's eye," a moody pool of light that has "intelligence with some remote horizon." Having perhaps already been in existence, he muses, when Adam and Eve fled the Garden of Eden, it has "obtained a patent of heaven to be the only Walden Pond and distiller of celestial dews."[6]

This "gem of the first water" is so full of light and reflections as to be a "lower heaven." Thoreau "cannot come nearer to God and Heaven" than to live by its shores. Spirits seemed to hover over its waters.[7]

> As the sun arose, I saw it throwing off its nightly clothing of mist, and here and there, by degrees, its soft ripples or its smooth reflecting surface was revealed, while the mists, like ghosts, were stealthily withdrawing in every direction into the woods, as at the breaking up of some nocturnal conventicle.[8]

He calls his bathing each morning "a religious exercise, and one of the best things which I did." At Walden, he did not merely read the classics; he "consecrated" his morning hours to them. And he passed hours in contemplation.[9]

A Way Out and a Way In

Thoreau was mired in a vocational crisis before Walden. Having failed to jump-start his literary career during his time on Staten Island in 1843, he returned to Concord to work in the family pencil business. He was both glad to be home and dispirited. He clamored "for one true vision," as he would later write in *A Week*. "But how can I communicate with the gods who am a pencil-maker on the earth, and not be insane?" Walden was his way out. Building his house there in the spring and summer of 1845 was like building a magic portal to another realm. But rather than ushering him into a fantasy world, it led Thoreau deeper into absolute reality— into the realm of sacred space and time. Although his dubious neighbors thought otherwise, Thoreau knew it was they, not he, who was living a life of illusion.[10]

"Both time and place were changed, and I dwelt nearer to those parts of the universe and to those eras in history which had most attracted me," Thoreau writes in *Walden*. "We are wont to imagine rare and delectable places in some remote and more celestial corner of the system. . . . I discovered that my house actually had its site in such a withdrawn, but forever new and unprofaned, part of the universe." Thoreau's wish to live in an "unprofaned" part of the universe suggests a central dichotomy in *Walden*, between the sacred and the profane. Thoreau strove to experience the sacred through spiritual practices, such as walking, meditation, close observation of nature, reading, keeping a journal, prayer, hoeing beans, and purifying his body through diet and bathing.[11]

Thoreau's reference to "delectable places" is one of several allusions to Christian imagery that is easy to miss. It refers to Bunyan's Christian allegory, *The Pilgrim's Progress*, which was among the most widely read books in Thoreau's day. In it, the paradigmatic pilgrim, named Christian, passes through many temptations and perils until he finally enters the heavenly Delectable Mountains, which overflow with gardens, orchards, vineyards, and fountains. In the opening chapter of *Walden*, Thoreau calls being in debt a "very ancient slough," which alludes to the sticky "slough of Despond" that Bunyan's pilgrim must pass through. Thoreau also takes a crack at a wealthy farmer by dubbing him "Squire Make-a-Stir," a name he makes up but which is similar in structure to the allegorical character names in *The Pilgrim's Progress*. "Some piece of mica, as it were," he wrote Blake in 1853, "as on the Delectable Mountains, slanted at the right angle, reflects the heavens to us."[12]

Thoreau's hardheaded, no-nonsense empiricism is one of the delights of *Walden*, but it never conflicts with his spiritual aims. He famously says his goal is to "drive life into a corner and reduce it to its lowest terms," and, if it proves to be mean, to get the whole meanness of it and publish it to the world. But he adds that if life proves sublime, he will "know it by experience, and be able to give a true account of it in my next excursion"—presumably, his next life. The passage is based on a *Journal* entry from July 6, 1845, two days after he began his Walden sojourn, that is even less Lockean in tone. "I wish to meet the facts of life—the vital facts, which were the phenomena or actuality the Gods meant to show us—face to face. And so I came down here." In *Walden* Thoreau declares that most men are uncertain about life, "whether it is of the devil or of God, and have *somewhat hastily* concluded that it is the chief end of man here to 'glorify God and enjoy him forever.'" Read one way, this sentence appears to question such an aim. But as his use of italics indicate, he is disagreeing with those who accept that purpose too quickly rather than by discovering it through personal experience.[13]

The sacredness and interconnection of all life, human and nonhuman, that Thoreau experienced at Walden also informed his economic and political critique of society. As Alda Balthrop-Lewis and others have noted, his simple, ascetic life at Walden looks like a withdrawal or renunciation only from the narrow perspective of the town road that runs past the pond. Living a contemplative life stripped to bare essentials, and writing forcefully and eloquently about what it taught him, was an act of resistance that connected him to others. "All health and success does me good, however far off and withdrawn it may appear," he wrote in *Walden*. "All disease and failure helps to make me sad and does me evil, however much sympathy it may have with me or I with it."[14]

It is no accident, for example, that the precipitating event behind "Civil Disobedience," Thoreau's refusal to pay a poll tax, occurred while he lived at Walden, and that he wrote the essay and the book almost concurrently. For Thoreau, following one's spiritual genius and following one's moral conscience entail the same dedication to simplicity, integrity, and faithfulness to an inner compass. Such a life releases time and energies that, rather than being spent on superficial ends, can be directed toward moral action and civic engagement. Would Thoreau even have refused to pay his poll tax in 1846 if, rather than moving to the pond, he had remained a worker in the family pencil business? Contemplation, his life shows, provides not only spiritual refreshment but a springboard to action.[15]

An Infinity of Springs

Thoreau went to live at Walden still grieving the loss of his brother three years earlier, and he was profoundly affected by the cycle of death and rebirth he witnessed there. The arrival of spring especially fortified his belief in an immortality that we may enjoy now if we align ourselves at the deepest level of consciousness with the wild. Each of us can experience a rebirth of our souls, he felt, just as the frozen pond melts under the inward warmth of the returning sun. This rebirth is a kind of wakefulness that the mere passage of the night cannot make to dawn.

Thoreau saw the natural world as Nature, with a capital *N*, and he believed it to be eternal. That view may seem quaint now in the Anthropocene, which some scientists date to 1945 and the first atomic bomb, a hundred years after Thoreau went to Walden. But in *Walden* Thoreau sees wildness as a remedial, regenerative, and spiritual force greater than anything we can do to it.

> The first sparrow of spring! The very beginning with younger hope than ever! . . . The grass flames up on the hillsides like a spring fire . . . as if the earth sent forth an inward heat to greet the returning sun; not yellow but green is the color of its flame—the symbol of perpetual youth, the grass blade, like a long green ribbon, streams from the sod into the summer, . . . lifting its spear of last year's hay with the fresh life below. . . . So our human life but dies down to its roots, and still puts forth its green blade to eternity.[16]

Comments Thoreau made in his final illness have raised the question of whether he believed in the personal immortality of the soul. As he lay dying, and his sister Sophia read to him from his account of his river trip with John, she heard him whisper, "Now comes good sailing." On May 5, 1862, the day before he died, his longtime friend, the farmer Edmund Hosmer, brought him news of robins singing. "This is a beautiful world," Thoreau is said to have replied, "but soon I shall see one that is fairer." He also famously parried his Aunt Louisa's request to make his peace with God by saying he was not aware that they had ever quarreled. Asked by the staunch abolitionist Parker Pillsbury shortly before his death how "the opposite shore" appeared to him, he replied, "One world at a time."[17]

That last quip aside, Thoreau's *Journal* makes clear that he had in fact been thinking about the opposite shore throughout his life. As we saw in chapter 1, in only his second *Journal* entry, at age 20, he wrote that the passing away of one life is the making room for another. Death is not final, not a cessation, but a phase in the cycles of nature, a law of life. This was the position Thoreau willed himself to accept with some difficulty after John died and which he later came to fully embrace. Two months after John's death, he wrote Emerson:

> How plain that death is only the phenomenon of the individual or class. Nature does not recognize it, She finds her own again under new forms without loss. Yet death is beautiful when seen to be a law, and not an accident. . . . Every blade in the field—every leaf in the forest—lays down its life in its season as beautifully as it was taken up. When we look over the fields we are not saddened because these particular flowers or grasses will wither—for the law of their death is the law of new life.[18]

Thoreau came to see his experience in nature, metaphorically, as only part of the journey of his soul. "May not my life in nature, in proportion as it is supernatural, be only the spring and infantile portion of my spirit's life?" he asked in his *Journal*. He vowed not to accept any substitute for the fullness of that journey. "May I not sacrifice a hasty and petty completeness here to an entireness there? If my curve is large, why bend it to a smaller circle?"[19]

The body, he knew, would be cast aside and plowed into the soil for compost. "No new life occupies the old bodies," he wrote Harrison Blake. "They decay." But he had faith that the soul had some vaguely understood but vital share in nature's cycles of renewal, that it would somehow emerge, transformed, into a more perfect state of harmony with the natural world and enjoy an eternity of springs.[20]

In March 1856, Thoreau returned to the Deep Cut, the site of the gestating sandbank that he wrote about in *Walden*, looking for any new life that the spring sun had called forth from the warm sandy soil. He saw none that day but was still reassured of nature's immortality and his own share of it.

> I am reassured and reminded that I am the heir of eternal inheritances which are inalienable, when I feel the warmth reflected from this sunny bank. . . . The eternity which I detect in Nature I predicate of myself also. How many springs I have had this same experience! I am encouraged, for I recognize this steady persistency and recovery of Nature as a quality of myself.[21]

Thoreau's faith in immortality was not confined to spring. It was stirred in October by the witch hazel, which blossoms as other trees are shedding leaves. "I love to be reminded of that universal and eternal spring when the minute crimson-starred female flowers of the hazel are peeping forth on the hillsides," he wrote, "when Nature revives in all her pores." And the sight of yellowed leaves and lily plants lying on the bottom of the Concord River in November reminded Thoreau, he said, "that nature is prepared for an infinity of springs."[22]

The historian of religion Mircea Eliade's study of the religious archetypes in the human psyche includes an analysis of sacred structures, natural or built. The threshold is the point at which one passes into sacred space, which always contains an axis that aligns it to the cosmos. It may be a roof pole, an open hole, or, outdoors, a tree connecting earth and heaven. It may also be a chimney, as it was in the house Thoreau built. In the evening, "when the villagers were lighting their fires beyond the horizon," he writes in the chapter "House-warming" in *Walden*, "I too gave notice to the various wild inhabitants of Walden vale, by a smoky streamer from my chimney, that I was awake." He then imagines the "light-winged smoke" that rises from his chimney as a silent lark and messenger of dawn "circling above the hamlets as thy nest." Then, in his mind's eye, the smoke is a departing dream, a shadowy form that veils the stars at night. His muse about his vaporous offering ends: "Go thou my incense upward from this hearth."[23]

as strange as it sounds. For one thing, both shared a distinctly Victorian view of these subjects. Blake, a former Unitarian minister, was one of the six graduating students (along with faculty and local ministers) before whom Emerson gave his Divinity School Address in 1838. He had met Thoreau at Emerson's house in 1844 and, based on an essay Thoreau wrote, revered him as a spiritual guru years before *Walden* appeared. As I mentioned in the introduction, Blake began their correspondence in 1848 by asking if the purpose of Thoreau's life was not to "sunder yourself from society, from the spell of institutions, customs and conventionalities, that you may lead a fresh, simple life with God." Blake also set the epistolary tone of their correspondence by asking of Thoreau, "Speak to me now at this hour as you are prompted."[4]

Most of Thoreau's fifty letters to Blake, which were written up through 1860 and shared by Blake with a coterie of Worcester followers, are mystical ruminations on the possibilities and pitfalls of living by the dictates of the soul. Many of the letters discuss the meaning of true work and offer a theology of vocation. As we saw in chapter 10, it was to Blake that Thoreau advised, "Let God alone if need be," adding that he was not sure "that that is the name. You will know whom I mean." If sometimes sermonic in tone, the letters are also personally revealing and spiritually edifying. They meant so much to Blake that, even on rereading them ten years later, he said, "in a sense they are still in the mail."[5]

Thoreau obliged Blake's request with a long essay describing love as a union of souls of such purity and sacredness as to be beyond speech. With characteristic hauteur, Thoreau said he would require anyone whom he loved to know everything about him without being told anything. "I parted from my beloved because there was one thing which I had to tell her," he wrote in an allegorical vein. "She questioned me. She should have known all by sympathy. That I had to tell it her was the difference between us."[6]

If Thoreau had been questioned about his religion, his response would likely have been similar. It was too profound, too sacred a secret to be explained. "There are some things which a man never speaks of, which are much finer kept silent about." Not that Thoreau *made* a secret of his religious sensibility. In ways subtle or overt, his religious lens on life infused his writing with spiritual depth, even on ostensibly secular topics such as simplicity or true economy. But Thoreau never clarified, systematized, or stated his religious views in propositional terms, which has led some readers to view him principally as a secular writer and thinker.[7]

The fact that true religion is something "a man never speaks of" does not necessarily prevent soulful sharing between people, as Thoreau shows in *Walden* when he tells of his experience of spending an afternoon in silence with a visitor. As he was building his house, an older man and expert fisherman came to watch the process (possibly, Thoreau speculated, because he expected the house to be for the convenience of fishermen). Thoreau was pleased when the man sat in the doorway to arrange his lines. Later, they went out in a boat, "but not many words passed between us, for he had grown deaf in his later years, but he occasionally hummed a psalm, which harmonized well enough with my philosophy. Our intercourse was thus altogether one of unbroken harmony, far more pleasing to remember than if it had been carried on by speech."[8]

Another reason for Thoreau's public silence on his deepest religious views was the inadequacy of words with which to speak them. Thoreau said there were more secrets in his trade than in most others, "and yet not voluntarily kept, but inseparable from its very nature." Poetic words convey the religious sentiment better than prose, but they are nonetheless inadequate. The truth overruns them. "The words which express our faith and piety are not definite," he writes in *Walden*. "I fear chiefly lest my expression may not be extravagant enough . . . to be adequate to the truth of which I have been convinced."[9]

The words we use to express our faith are "volatile" because they are heard differently by different persons. "Their truth is instantly translated; its literal monument [the words used to express it] alone remains." Again Thoreau's thought aligns here with that of his mentor. "All symbols are fluctional [in flux]" and "all language is vehicular and transitive," Emerson wrote in his essay "The Poet," "and is good, as ferries and horses are, for conveyance, not as farms and houses are, for homestead."[10]

The Silence Rings

Silence was more than the absence of speech for Thoreau. It had a spiritual texture and resonance, which he described as an "undercurrent" to sound. Sound is an emissary that alerts us to the silence behind it. It is a "bubble on her surface," he wrote in 1838, "which straightaway bursts, an emblem of the strength and prolifickness of the undercurrent." Silence is the solemn universal canvas or musical staff on which all sound is scored. But it is only human sounds that disrupt it; those of nature do not. The rushing, flapping sound of a flock of starlings pivoting in flight, or the tapping of a nuthatch on the trunk of a pine or hemlock, Thoreau wrote, do not disturb the silence so much as amplify and intensify it.[11]

Silence deepened his thought, as when he felt soothed by the stillness of an August evening as he sat at sunset atop Bittern Cliff overlooking Fair Haven Bay. "The din of trivialness

is silenced. I float over or through the deeps of silence. It is
the first silence I have heard for a month. My life had been a
River Platte, tinkling over its sands but useless for all great
navigation, but now it suddenly became a fathomless ocean.
It shelved off to unimagined depths."[12]

Thoreau draped silence in religious imagery. Thunder is
but a warning "that we may know what communion awaits
us" in the silence to follow, he wrote in his *Journal*. "Not its
dull sound, but the infinite expansion of our being which en-
sues, we praise and unanimously name sublime." Silence expanded Thoreau's awareness—not of any particular thing, but
of awareness itself, of the life poring through his veins and
throbbing around him. That "infinite expansion" of his soul
led him on a path of spiritual discovery.[13]

Thoreau ends *A Week* with a long passage on the spiritual nature of silence that concludes, "As the truest society
approaches always nearer to solitude, so the most excellent
speech finally falls into Silence. Silence is audible to all men,
at all times, in all places." The passage is drawn from an 1838
Journal entry in which he wrote, "Silence is the communing of
a conscious soul with itself. If the soul attends for a moment
to its own infinity, then and there is silence. She is audible to
all men, at all times, in all places."[14]

Thoreau does not invoke God or the divine mystery in that
1838 passage. Instead he capitalizes "Silence" and paints it
as the primordial material of which all is made and through
which "all revelations are made." It existed before the first wind
swept over the waters. "Silence *was*, say we, before ever the
world was, as if creation had displaced her, and were not her
visible framework and foil." Although seemingly displaced by
creation, the solemn stillness of the original silence can still
be heard by the inward ear today. Truth, goodness, and beauty

make audible "Her infinite din," and a good book is the plectrum, or pick, "with which our else silent lyres are struck."[15]

Silence is "the universal refuge," "our inviolable asylum," and "that background which the painter may not daub." If religion is indeed that which is not spoken, it originates in silence. "It were vain for me to endeavor to interpret the Silence," Thoreau wrote in the conclusion to *A Week*—as vain as the banner stretched across the Concord house in 1858. "She cannot be done into English. For six thousand years men have translated her with what fidelity belonged to each, and still she is little better than a sealed book." Thoreau did not literally accept the still popular belief that the world was only six thousand years old, which James Ussher, a seventeenth-century Irish archbishop and scholar, had calculated in 1650. Thoreau's point is that whatever the age of Earth, no one has ever unsealed that "book" (silence) which is both source and sequel to the Bible. Silence is the great "untold."[16]

> A man may run on confidently for a time, thinking he has her under his thumb, and shall one day exhaust her, but he too must at last be silent, and men remark only how brave a beginning he made; for when he at length dives into her, so vast is the disproportion of the told to the untold, that the former will seem but the bubble on the surface where he disappeared.[17]

Silence is ultimate depth—the hard bottom in nature that he could not put his foot through, and which he wrote in *Walden* that he craved. It is something positive to be heard. It is, he writes, a realm in which it is possible to hear unspoken sounds with new ears. In 1853, he left the village one summer night to commune with it.

I must stand still and listen with open ears, far from the
noises of the village, that the night may make its impression on me. . . . As I leave the village, drawing nearer to
the woods, I listen from time to time to hear the hounds of
Silence baying the Moon—to know if they are on the track
of any game. . . . The silence rings; it is musical and thrills
me. A night in which the silence was audible. I hear the
unspeakable.[18]

Thoreau coined one of his more creative metaphors for
silence in an 1854 letter to Blake. He wrote that he left his
house one August night in search of any "depth of silence"
and paddled up the Sudbury River to a quiet cove. There he
imagined the "shallow din" of the world as a kind of creature
he drowned amid the still evening on the water. The expansion of being he described is characteristic of his spiritual
experience.

As Bonaparte sent out his horsemen in the Red Sea on all
sides to find shallow water, so I sent forth my mounted
thoughts to find deep water. I left the village and paddled up
the river to Fair Haven Pond. . . . The falling dews seemed
to strain and purify the air, and I was smoothed with an
infinite stillness. I got the world, as it were, by the nape of
the neck, and held it under in the tide of its own events,
till it was drowned, and then I let it go down-stream like a
dead dog. Vast hollow chambers of silence stretched away
on every side, and my being expanded in proportion, and
filled them.[19]

Thoreau's cringing response to the house blaring its owner's
faith in God on the occasion of the transatlantic telegraph is

similar to his response to conventional moralism. The moral sentiment is about living in right relation to the human and more-than-human world. That principle was sacrosanct with Thoreau, who was a champion of the higher law. But he was a fierce opponent of the moralism hurrahed by the church because it was prescribed externally by dogma and tradition rather than by experience and intuition. The conventional moralism of his society was, to Thoreau, a kind of noise that separates us from a fresh, original relation to life—from what he called "the very vitality of vita." The person who knows that vitality does not require a banner to proclaim it.

> Occasionally we rise above the necessity of virtue into
> an unchangeable morning light, in which we have not to
> choose in a dilemma between right and wrong, but simply
> to live right on and breathe the circumambient air. There
> is no name for this life unless it be the very vitality of vita.
> Silent is the preacher about this, and silent must ever be, for
> he who knows it will not preach.[20]

SIXTEEN

"A Place beyond All Place"

Although the creativity of Thoreau's religious thought and its centrality to his life's work is increasingly being recognized by scholars, he did not leave a clearly marked or easy-to-follow spiritual path for others. Indeed, his spirituality is characterized by a series of baffling paradoxes. He was a deeply religious person without a religion. He rejected the "personality" of God but at times portrayed a personal creator. He was an ultraradical reformer who held a sacramental view of nature. He saw historical Christianity as a failure but framed his religious views in its poetry and verse. He said, "Our spirits never go beyond nature," and he also said we "must look through and beyond her." He so loved the earth that he looked forward to being buried in its soil, yet he alluded to heaven, as a metaphor, literally hundreds of times in his *Journal*.[1]

Perhaps the central paradox is that last one—the tension between Thoreau's palpable love of this green earth and his anticipation of and yearning for a mystical dimension of reality that he describes variously as another world or another kind of life.

In a letter to Harrison Blake in November 1857 about the spiritual aspects of mountain climbing, Thoreau paused to describe another kind of ascent he sometimes made.

> I keep a mountain anchored off eastward a little way, which I ascend in my dreams both awake and asleep. Its broad base spreads over a village or two, which does not know it; neither does it know them, nor do I when I ascend it. I can see its general outline as plainly now in my mind as that of Wachusett. I do not invent in the least, but state exactly what I see. I find that I go up it when I am light-footed and earnest. It ever smokes like an altar with its sacrifice. I am not aware that a single villager frequents it or knows of it. I keep this mountain to ride instead of a horse.[2]

What is this personal peak Thoreau has stashed in the eastern sky? Although it smokes like an altar, the village at its base does not know that it exists. Thoreau can see it plainly in his mind's eye, but he has no actual, factual knowledge of it. He ascends it when he feels "light-footed and earnest" but also in his dreams—and in the day as well as at night. He rides it like a horse, carried along on its back perhaps the way the wind filled his boat's sails on the river. One wonders if he has found the bay horse whose loss he famously mourns in *Walden*.

The mountain expresses Thoreau's strong mystical streak, his consciousness of a mysterious place or state of being that he speaks of wistfully as a "distant shore," "that other world," "your land of promise," and "that other kind of life to which I am continually allured." The actual world seemed less real to him than this intuited one, he wrote Blake on March 27, 1848.[3]

> This, our respectable daily life, on which the man of common sense, the Englishman of the world, stands so squarely,

and on which our institutions are founded, is in fact the veriest illusion, and will vanish like the baseless fabric of a vision; but that faint glimmer of reality which sometimes illuminates the darkness of daylight for all men, reveals something more solid and enduring than adamant, which is in fact the cornerstone of the world.[4]

And two years later, in his *Journal*: "We are ever dying to one world and being born into another."[5]

Emerson alluded to this side of Thoreau in his eulogy. "In his youth, he said, one day, 'The other world is all my art: my pencils will draw no other; my jack-knife will cut nothing else; I do not use it as a means.' This was the muse and genius that ruled his opinions, conversation, studies, work, and course of life."[6]

That description accords with the Thoreau who wrote of his two years and two months at Walden Pond: "There too, as everywhere, I sometimes expected the Visitor who never comes." Other than the capitalizing *Visitor*, Thoreau gives no hint whom he was expecting.[7]

Thoreau's other world imagery suggests that he knew of the mystics East and West who over the centuries have affirmed that "this world" is illusory and transient and that we can awake to the real and permanent through prayer and contemplation. In fact, Thoreau's ideas seem to have arisen largely from his own mystical experience and reflection, not his reading. He took his own path of unknowing to arrive at the same place (or no place) as Hasidic, Zen, Sufi, Hindu, and Christian mystics of lore.

Thoreau refers to this dimension repeatedly in *A Week*. The book opens with an epigraph to his brother, John, whom he calls "the only permanent shore" and "the cape never rounded." It includes the lines:

I am bound, I am bound, for a distant shore.
By a lonely isle, by a far Azore,
There it is, there it is, the treasure I seek,
On the barren islands of a desolate creek.[8]

In the book's final chapter, as the October sun is falling behind a flaming ridge of trees, Thoreau sees "portals to other mansions" than those in which we live—a possible reference to John 14:2, "In my Father's house are many mansions." These mansions are "not far off geographically," Thoreau tells us, but are in "a place beyond all place."[9]

And *A Week* ends with a long mediation about the existence of "another and purer realm" on the outskirts of which we live. After noting that Galileo discovered that Venus is "another world, in itself," and not merely, as previously thought, a satellite of the earth, Thoreau writes, "I am not without hope that we may, even here and now obtain some accurate information concerning that OTHER WORLD which the instinct of mankind has so long predicted." (The capitalization is Thoreau's.)[10]

Adrift in the World

Thoreau's glimpses of that other world stirred an indefinable yearning that sometimes left him feeling not at home in this one. "The society which I was made for is not here," he wrote in 1851. He speaks of going "on a solitary woodland walk as the homesick go home." A golden sunset in a pine grove evoked that restless feeling.[11]

Looking through a stately pine grove, I saw the western sun falling in golden streams through its aisles. Its west side, opposite to me, was all lit up with golden light; but what was I to it? Such sights remind me of houses which we never inhabit, that commonly I am not at home in the world. I see somewhat fairer than I enjoy or possess.[12]

Thoreau even described himself as "homeless" to Blake. One letter begins—responding to an unknown topic suggested by his Worcester correspondent—"Another singular kind of spiritual foot ball—really nameless, handleless, homeless, like myself."[13]

Thoreau suggests we must choose which "world" to inhabit, and he vows not to accept a hasty and "desperate" substitute for his "heaven." That is what he did at Walden by renouncing the conventional life of his neighbors and their pursuit of superficialities. And it is the meaning behind his famous line in *Walden* about marching to a different drummer.

If a man does keep pace with his companions, perhaps it is because he hears a different drummer. Let him step to the music which he hears, however measured or far away. . . . If the condition of things which we were made for is not yet, what were any reality which we can substitute? We will not be shipwrecked on a vain reality. Shall we with pains erect a heaven of blue glass over ourselves, though when it is done we shall be sure to gaze still at the true ethereal heaven far above, as if the former were not?[14]

At Home in Nature

This is admittedly hard to square with the more familiar, earthbound Thoreau who, as he also makes abundantly clear, *was* at home in nature, who called the solid, sunny earth "the basis of all philosophy, poetry and religion" and who saw nature as the source of physical, mental, and spiritual health.

Thoreau had no patience with people who, disappointed with this world, looked to the next one for compensation.[15]

> One of little faith looks for his rewards and punishments to the next world, and, despairing of this world, behaves accordingly in it; another thinks the present a worthy occasion and arena, sacrifices to it, and expects to hear sympathizing voices. The man who believes in another world and not in this is wont to put me off with Christianity.[16]

Thoreau's devotion to the earth is no less strong than his mysticism. "You must love the crust of the earth on which you dwell more than the sweet crust of any bread or cake." Heaven is here or nowhere, Thoreau believed, and he vowed to love the common and the everyday so that "I may dream of no heaven but that which lies about me." Visiting Lake Cochituate in nearby Natick, Massachusetts, Thoreau saw "the naked flesh of New England" exposed on its "glorious sandy shores" and was enraptured. "Of thee, O earth, are my bone and sinew made," he wrote. "Here I have my habitat. I am of thee." Thoreau inhabited his own body as well as the soil of his homeland. Surely he would have understood what the twentieth-century Scottish nature writer Nan Shepherd meant when she wrote, in *The Living Mountain*, "The body is not made negligible but paramount. Flesh is not annihilated but fulfilled. One is not bodiless, but essential body."[17]

A World Within

The mountain Thoreau kept anchored in the sky did not conflict, however, with his terranean passion. The two worlds were flip sides of the same reality. Thoreau used spatial and temporal metaphors to express his mystical yearnings the same way he used figurative language to write about God without accepting the finality or literal meaning of his words. Thoreau's other world is not really another place. And it is not a *next* world. There is another world, Thoreau tells us, but it is hidden in the heart of this one, so familiar and yet so strange to us. It is the inner continent that only the bravest explorer discovers, and not all at once in a grand eureka moment, but slowly, with patience and discipline. The "other world" is revealed through a truer perception of this one. The fibrous blue spikes of the aquatic pickerel weed, reflected in the Concord River, point "down to a heaven beneath as well as above."[18]

Thoreau wrote in a letter to Blake that the inward and outward life correspond and that spirit and matter are one. "The outward is only the outside of that which is in." And shortly before *Walden* was published, he wrote in his *Journal*, "This earth which is spread out like a map around me is but the lining of my inmost soul exposed."[19]

It is easier to discover a new physical world, such as the great explorers did, "than to go within one fold of this *which we appear to know so well*," Thoreau writes in *A Week* (emphasis added.) We are so keyed to the sensate world and to the personal identities we construct that Thoreau's suggestion is hard to put into practice. Our compasses fail, we get lost, our inner crew mutinies, and we end up stranded amid the rubbish of history. We fail—but not completely. "There is only necessary a moment's sanity and sound senses, to teach us that there is a nature behind the ordinary. . . . We live on the outskirts of that region. Carved wood, and floating boughs, and sunset skies, are all that we know of it." Still we must seek it, Thoreau tells us in *Walden*. "Be a Columbus," he writes, "to whole new continents and worlds within you."[20]

This nature beyond the ordinary is the balmy "distant

shore" to which God, the "skillful pilot," ferries the Irish immigrants who drowned in the wreck of the *St. John*—that world we may know, not through our logical faculties, but through "a continual drift and instinct to all our shores." Thoreau offers that triumphal image of deliverance in *Cape Cod* as metaphor, not theology. Neither do our bodies need to toss in the surf to get there. We may reach this halcyon land if we develop our inner compass enough to find it in the here and now. The world of our everyday lives can be a source of spiritual renewal if we learn to see the ordinary in extraordinary ways and attend to it with devotion. Attention will lead to ascension.[21]

Thoreau experienced this inner world at age 24, when he heard the church bell ring and felt the past and present fused. He was writing some of his most important poems then, and the note of lost innocence in his reflection shows Wordsworth's influence on him. "When I hear this bell ring, I am carried back to years and Sabbaths when I was newer and more innocent, I fear, than now, and it seems to me as if there were a world within a world."[22]

Although this insight into the unity of the material and the spiritual was sharpened by Thoreau's later natural history studies, he had been introduced to it by age 18 by Orestes Brownson, the Unitarian minister with whom he lived while on a break from Harvard to teach in Canton (then a rural town south of Boston) in late 1835 and early 1836. A religious radical and leading Transcendentalist thinker, Brownson rejected the Pauline distinction between matter and spirit, embraced universal salvation, and sought to make Unitarianism a religion for the masses, though he would later become a Catholic. Central to his philosophy, as we saw in chapter 2, was a "doctrine of atonement" that held "that spirit is real and holy, that matter is real and holy, that God is holy and that man is holy." Thoreau absorbed that belief in his sophomore year at Harvard and never shed it.[23]

Going Out and Going In

Late in life, John Muir reflected on his life out of doors. "I only went out for a walk," he wrote, "and finally concluded to stay out till sundown, for going out, I found, was really going in." Something similar was true for Thoreau in his later years. Going out into nature and studying its cycles and processes became a way of going to the divinity within. Thoreau had forecast the direction his life's work would take in a poem, "The Thaw," which he wrote five years after his time with Brownson. In it he aspires to flow through nature's very pores:[24]

> Fain would I stretch me by the highway side,
> To thaw and trickle with the melting snow,
> That mingled soul and body with the tide,
> I too may through the pores of nature flow.[25]

Thoreau reflected on religion less often in his later *Journal* as his natural history studies intensified, just as he reflected less on art, society, and literature than he did in the 1840s and early 1850s. His *Journal* was still a mix of such subjective musings and observations of nature, but the balance shifted toward his observation and recording of natural phenomena. Thoreau did not become a disenchanted materialist in his later years, however, as has been well established by scholars including Lawrence Buell, Alan Hodder, David Robinson, Laura Dassow Walls, and Malcolm Clemens Young. He never stopped contemplating the relationship between the natural and the metaphysical. Buell wrote that Thoreau's deeper immersion in the natural world represented an evolution of, not a break with, his youthful Transcendentalism. The image of a Thoreau who cast the residues of theism and pantheism behind him, he wrote, should up to a point "be seen as a progression rather than a decline—a fulfillment more complete."[26]

"The fact will one day flower into a truth," Thoreau had written in his first notebook in 1837. "The season will mature and fructify what the understanding has cultivated." To merely accumulate dry facts was pointless. When a farmer offered him, as a naturalist, a two-headed calf that had been born at his farm, Thoreau was appalled. He was not interested in "mere phenomena" for its own sake. As he indicated in his essay "Autumnal Tints," a meditation on death and resurrection in nature, and his extensive reflections on seeds and fruits, he was not just accumulating facts in his natural history studies.[27]

Having concluded that matter is holy, studying it became an act of contemplation and veneration. Thoreau's religious sensibility overlapped with his close identification and continuity with all forms of life. He felt less need to restate his ideas about religion because he had already worked them out. His focus became putting them into practice. As he studied marigolds, for example, his materialism was his mysticism. His field work and his spiritual quest were motivated by a desire to "detect the *anima* or soul in every thing."[28]

Indeed, science itself discloses a universal intelligence, Thoreau wrote. A human skeleton may at first elicit a shudder, but on calm examination it becomes simply a natural object. "We discover that the only spirit which haunts it is a Universal Intelligence which has created it in harmony with all nature. Science never saw a ghost, nor does it look for any, but it sees everywhere the traces, and is itself the agent, of a Universal Intelligence."[29]

Religion in the Late *Journal*

What is less well known is that Thoreau's episodes of exhilaration, his comments on the spiritual meaning of natural phenomena, and his references to God continued to appear in his later *Journal*. Such remarks become sparse from 1853 through late 1857; then there is a resurgence of them from late 1857 through December 1859. They again decline, only to resurface as he faced death, in spring 1862, when Thoreau spoke with serene confidence and even cheerfulness about the prospect of seeing a fairer world than this one.

His *Journal* entries in 1858, 1859, and 1860 provide a telling example. "I may say that the maker of the world exhausts his skill with each snowflake and dewdrop that he sends down," he wrote in January 1858. Snowflakes are "the product of enthusiasm, the children of an ecstasy, finished with the artist's utmost skill." Later that same month, a rainfall lifted Thoreau's spirits with its signs of immortality. Deprivation, as ever, was his daffodil.[30]

> A rain which is as serene as fair weather, suggesting fairer weather than was ever seen. You could hug the clods that defile you. You feel the fertilizing influence of the rain in your mind. The part of you that is wettest is fullest of life, like the lichens. You discover evidences of immortality not known to divines. You cease to die. You detect some buds and sprouts of life.[31]

In April 1858, he doubted "if men do ever simply and naturally glorify God in the ordinary sense, but it is remarkable how sincerely in all ages they glorify nature."[32]

On November 20, 1858, he mused that people deemed religious are more conservative, timid, and "useless" than others and that they blaspheme God's name. "Instead of going bravely about their business, trusting God ever, they do like him who says 'Good sir' to the one he fears, or whistles to the dog that is rushing at him. And because they take his name in vain so often they presume that they are better than you. Oh their religion is a rotten squash."

Ten days later, on November 30, 1858, he saw a bream, a type of fish, as a spiritual symbol. "The bream, appreciated"—that is, seen truly and attentively—"floats in the pond as the centre of the system, another image of God."

In January 1859, as we saw in chapter 9, he compared God to a mother who loves see her children thrive. In March he said the mysterious life of plants can only be understood from a "reverent" perspective.

> We must not expect to probe with our fingers the sanctuary of any life, whether animal or vegetable. If we do, we shall discover nothing but surface still. The ultimate expression or fruit of any created thing is a fine effluence which only the most ingenuous worshipper perceives at a reverent distance from its surface even. The cause and the effect are equally evanescent and intangible, and the former must be investigated in the same spirit and with the same reverence with which the latter is perceived. . . . Shall we presume to alter the angle at which God chooses to be worshipped?[33]

Thoreau reworked that passage in his late project *Wild Fruits*, adding: "There is no ripeness which is not, so to speak, something ultimate in itself, and not merely a perfected means to what we believe a higher end. In order to be ripe it must serve a transcendent use. The ripeness of the leaf being perfected (for aught we know), it leaves the tree at that point and never returns to it. . . . Only genius can pluck it."[34]

Ferns as a "Sacred Scripture"

In October 1859, Thoreau said that in order to be affected by a plant, you must forget your botany. It is a simple matter to learn the physical characteristics if a fern, for example, he wrote; a scientific description will do for that. "But if it is required that you be affected by ferns," that they mean anything to you, "that they be another sacred scripture and revelation to you, helping to redeem your life, this end is not so surely accomplished."[35]

Thoreau voiced his Transcendentalism again in January 1860 as he followed a crow in flight. (A "tympanum" is a resonating membrane, like the eardrum, as well as the name of a musical instrument.) "The crow, flying high, touches the tympanum of the sky for us, and reveals the tone of it. What does it avail to look at a thermometer or barometer compared with listening to his note?"[36]

On February 12, 1860, Thoreau sauntered over a frozen Fair Haven Pond in late afternoon. As the sun began to set, the patches of flat snow in the shadows on the pond reflected a purple tinge—"a most beautiful crystalline purple, like the petals of some flowers, or as if tinged with cranberry juice. It is quite a faery scene, surprising and wonderful, as if you walked amid those rosy and purple clouds that you see float in the evening sky." That the purple patches of snow mirrored the color of the clouds led Thoreau to muse on the affinity between heaven and earth.

> This is but a sunset sky under our feet, produced by the same law, the same slanting rays and twilight. . . . Thus all

of heaven is realized on earth. You have seen those purple
fortunate isles in the sunset heavens, and that green and
amber sky between them. Would you believe that you could
ever walk amid those isles? You can on many a winter
evening. I have done so a hundred times. The ice is a solid
crystalline sky under our feet.

Six days later, on February 18, Thoreau thought the most
important thing to know about an animal is its spirit.

I think that the most important requisite in describing an
animal, is to be sure and give its character and spirit, for
in that you have, without error, the sum and effect of all its
parts, known and unknown. You must tell what it is to man.
Surely the most important part of an animal is its *anima*, its
vital spirit, on which is based its character and all the pecu-
liarities by which it most concerns us.

On December 4, 1860, two days after he contracted the cold
that would lead to his death, he wrote in his Indian notebooks
that Christianity never matches its ideal. "When the husk gets
separated from the kernel, almost all men run after the husk
and pay their respects to that. It is only the husk of Christianity that is so bruited and wide spread in this world, the kernel
is still the very least and rarest of all things. There is not a
single church founded on it." It was four months later, as we
saw in chapter 9, that he wrote Parker Pillsbury that those
who do not read newspapers "will see Nature, and, through
her, God."[37]

Thoreau's devotion in his later *Journal* to understanding and
recording natural phenomena does not by itself indicate a
loss of spiritual energies, Alan Hodder has written. "If any-

thing, it suggests only a redirection, and perhaps intensifi-
cation, of energies evident in his early life." Hodder is right
that, even in his later years, Thoreau "was still animated by a
devotion and a sense of nature's mystery that can at its source
be conceived of in religious terms."[38]

SEVENTEEN

Thoreau's Refining Fire

On his last trip to Maine, Thoreau's guide, Joe Polis, asked him how he spent his Sundays, meaning did he go to church. He replied that he read in the morning and walked in the afternoon. This drew a mild reprimand from the Penobscot Indian, who said he went to church. "He stated that he was a Protestant, and asked me if I was. I did not at first know what to say, but I thought that I could answer with truth that I was."[1]

Thoreau disclosed his religion in his first reply, because reading and walking were spiritual practices for him. His aversion to any religious label likely accounts for the note of doubt in his second answer, but I think Thoreau spoke a less obvious truth there as well. Thoreau saw nature through the lens of his Puritan inheritance perhaps more than he was aware or willing to admit. More to the point, he was an extreme reformer, radical in his pursuit of spiritual truth. He scorned philanthropy and social reform in his day for being insufficiently radical but admired history's true reformers. We should listen to the "earnest reprovers of the age," he said. Even if they are fanatics, it "may be they who will put

to rest the American Church and the American government,
and awaken better ones in their stead." Emerson understood
this side of Thoreau when, in his eulogy, he called him both
"a born protestant" and "a protestant *à outrance*," or to the utmost, to the bitter end.[2]

The intent of the Puritan reformers was to strip the Angli-
can Church of elements they considered idolatrous or too material, such as the sacraments, the priesthood, and the veneration of saints. They believed that the yearning for God in the
human soul, stirred by reading the Bible, exceeds whatever
can be attained through material religion. *Sola scriptura*, by
scripture alone, are we saved. Thoreau was faithful to their instinct, but he did the reformers one better, omitting not only
those things they found offensive but also the church itself
as mediator between the human and divine. One could know
God, he believed, *sola naturae*, by nature alone.

Thoreau was a religious reformer in arguing that revelation is not a closed book. It is ever new, never finished, always
taking new forms. It cannot be reduced to one formulation or
contained in one religion. "There is always a later edition of
every book than the printer wots [knows] of, no matter how
recently it was published," he wrote in 1841. "All nature is a
new impression every instant."

Such impressions are especially fresh, he wrote a dozen
years later, on "mornings of creation," by which he means not
only the actual daybreak outside but also the morning inside
us, which, as he tells us in *Walden*, the mere passage of time
cannot make to dawn.

> There are from time to time mornings, both in summer
> and winter, when especially the world seems to begin
> anew, beyond which memory need not go. . . . Mornings
> of creation, I call them. . . . I look back for the era of this

creation, not into the night, but to a dawn for which no man ever rose early enough. A morning which carries us back beyond the Mosaic creation, where crystallizations are fresh and unmelted. It is the poet's hour. Mornings when men are newborn, men who have the seeds of life in them. It should be a part of my religion to [be] abroad then.[3]

However inspiring we may find Thoreau's account of being abroad then, it must remain for us, if we are faithful to his advice, a secondhand report. Unless our own philosophy hears the cock crow at every barnyard around us each day, as he wrote in "Walking," it is belated. If there are no roosters or barnyards near us, we must look for other chanticleers, other cock-a-doodle-doos to wake us up.

The Love Untold

At the core of Thoreau's religious vision was his desire to commune with sacred mystery. His Harvard classmate John Weiss may have been referring to this when he said he knew of no writer more penetrated with "the spiritualizing effect of a personal consciousness of God." Thoreau believed that such an experience requires the mental habit of attention. But it is also an affair of the heart, he tells us. Whether you love Christ or Buddha made no difference to him, "for the love is the main thing," as he wrote in *A Week*. "The religion I love is very laic," for it is "as unpublic and incommunicable as our poetical vein—and to be approached with as much love and tenderness." There was much tenderness, compassion, and love in Thoreau's religion.[4]

As I noted about Thoreau's remarks on Chaucer in chapter 11, he found affection for God rare in English letters. "No sentiment is so rare as love of God—universal love," he wrote.

Love of God meant just that to Thoreau: universal, transcendent love, love of life itself, love of the totality of creation, love of the moral law, and love of being alive in a universe we cannot explain but can only accept with gratitude and deep sympathy for all the life it contains. "It is the love of virtue makes us young ever," he said. "That is the fountain of youth. . . . I love and worship myself with a love which absorbs my love for the world."[5]

To love something was integral to Thoreau's religious vision because it is the essence of being fully alive. "All that a man has to say or do that can possibly concern mankind, is in some shape or other to tell the story of his love—to sing; and, if he is fortunate and keeps alive, he will be forever in love. This alone is to be alive to the extremities."[6]

Thoreau makes an odd apostle of love. He did not write about romantic love, except in the high-minded Victorian essay he wrote for Harrison Blake about love as a communion of souls, a union that is "as much a light as a flame." It is an open question to what extent Thoreau's transcendental ideal of friendship or agape compensated for the more personal disappointments of his heart, his unfulfilled yearning for a deeper bond with Emerson and his unrequited feelings for Ellen Sewell, to whom he is said to have professed his love on his deathbed. But there is no question that he desired love. "What if I feel a yearning to which no breast answers?" Thoreau wrote during a long bout of depression in 1855. "I walk alone. My heart is full. I would fain walk on the deep waters, but my companions will only walk in shadows and puddles." Ignorance and bungling with love are better than wisdom and skill without, he also wrote. "Our life without love is like coke and ashes." True aloneness, he thought, was not being close enough to another person to see the divinity in him or her.[7]

Thoreau's quest for religious truth was individual, but that did not make it solely interior or private. Indeed, it gave him a sense of the unity of all life through a web of reciprocal relationships governed by the moral law. In that sense his faith was inseparable from his ethical commitments and political stands. God, he wrote his friend Isaiah Thornton Williams, does not make us solitary agents. "Is our life innocent enough? Do we live *inhumanely*, toward man or beast, in thought or act?" he asked in his *Journal*. "To be serene and successful we must be at one with the universe. The least conscious & needless injury inflicted on any creature is to its extent a suicide."[8]

Thoreau famously wrote in *Walden* of losing a hound, a bay horse, and a turtledove; but most of that much-dissected passage in *Walden*, rather than mourning the loss, is about his experience of *sharing* the loss with others. "Many are the travelers I have spoken concerning them, describing their tracks and what calls they answered to. I have met one or two who have heard the hound, and the tramp of the horse, and even seen the dove disappear behind a cloud, and they seemed as anxious to recover them as if they had lost them themselves." By mythologizing his experience, Thoreau made it common.[9]

It was an unavoidable result of his process, and not his goal, that his spiritual path was solitary, he told Blake. "It is not that we love to be alone, but that we love to soar, and when we do soar, the company grows thinner and thinner till there is none at all. It is either the Tribune on the plain, a sermon on the mount, or a very private ecstasy still higher up. We are not the less to aim at the summits, though the multitude does not ascend them."[10]

To love another person, Thoreau said, is "to stand in true relation to him" and to "reflect a ray of God" to that person, he wrote in *A Week*. It anticipates that "fair, fresh and eternal" world within a world. Even grander and more mysterious than human love is communion with God, Thoreau wrote in his poem "Inspiration":[11]

> Be but thy inspiration given,
> No matter through what danger sought,
> I'll fathom hell or climb to heaven,
> And yet esteem that cheap which love has bought.[12]

The poem then speaks of the "love untold." The "untold" is a motif in Thoreau's writing for an all-enveloping love that is deeper than a love that needs to be told or expressed. It is the love we trust is there for us, if only by intuition, hope, and prayer. Being convicted of such a love, Thoreau will not break faith with it.

> I will not doubt the love untold
> Which not my worth nor want has bought,
> Which wooed me young, and woos me old,
> And to this evening hath me brought.

Knocking at the Door

When I think of Thoreau's characteristic religious posture, I think of him as an aspirant, a supplicant, a mendicant recusant, whose withdrawal from one kind of life was a means of actively pursuing another kind. He stood at the door of mystery and knocked. It was a mostly solitary path, but it also led him into kinship with all living beings, plant, animal and human—a way of seeing that makes "the very atoms bloom" into flowers. The important thing, he says, is to be on a path, to be building up a life. Thoreau was on such a path on New Year's Day 1854. He was in the woods after a great snowstorm, and the scene suggested to him a world of virtue, justice, purity, courage, and magnanimity. Hunters were also out that day, but Thoreau was on the trail of more than game. His *Journal* account is one of his most hauntingly beautiful passages about his lifelong pilgrimage to the holy land all around him.[13]

> Does not all this amount to the track of a higher life than the otter's, a life which has not gone by and left a footprint merely, but is there with its beauty, its music, its perfume, its sweetness, to exhilarate and recreate us? Where there is a perfect government of the world according to the highest laws, is there no trace of intelligence there, whether in the snow or the earth, or in ourselves? No other trail but such as a dog can smell? Is there none which an angel can detect and follow? None to guide a man on his pilgrimage which water will not conceal? Is there no odor of sanctity to be perceived?[14]

The key to being on the trail of some higher life, he continues, is to be alert enough to detect its traces in the snow. Such a person sees more than the track of some timorous hare. To that person is revealed traces "of the Great Hare, whose track no hunter has seen."[15]

> Are there not hunters who seek for something higher than foxes, with judgment more discriminating than the sense of foxhounds, who rally to a nobler music than that of the hunting horn? . . . He who would make the most of his life for a discipline, must be abroad early and late, in spite of cold and wet, in pursuit of nobler game, whose traces then are most distinct. A life which, pursued, does not earth itself, does not burrow downward but upward, which takes not to the trees but to the heavens as its home, which the

hunter pursues with winged thoughts and aspirations—
these the dogs that tree it—rallying his pack with the bugle
notes of undying faith, and returns with some trophy wor-
thier than a fox's tail, a life which we seek, not to destroy it,
but to save our own.[16]

How to put together the puzzle of Thoreau's religion? As we
have seen, perception of and attention to the sacred is at its
heart—seeing the soul, or *anima*, in everything, as Thoreau
put it. He understood, as Simone Weil, the French philosopher and Jewish–Catholic mystic, wrote, that "the value of
a religious or, more generally, a spiritual way of life is the
amount of illumination thrown upon the things of this world."
We may also say that, for Thoreau, religion is a matter of who
we are and how we live—in particular, whether we act justly
toward all life, human and nonhuman. And what matters
more than any one faith is an attitude of faithfulness.[17]

Thoreau does give a rare direct clue to the puzzle himself,
however, in a letter on September 8, 1841, to Isaiah Thornton
Williams, the young man who boarded at the Thoreau home
in Concord that year to learn about Transcendentalism and
who became his friend. "The strains of a more heroic faith
vibrate through the week days and the fields than through
the sabbath and the church," he wrote Williams. "To shut the
ears to the immediate voice of God, and prefer to know him
by report will be the only sin. . . . Our religion is where our
love is."[18]

Love, for Thoreau, was his desire to embrace and be embraced by something both within and without him, an energy as ceaselessly generative as the waves that lap upon that
other world, that distant shore—a wildness, a benevolence,
and a love that he often understood as God. As a literary art-

ist striving for language appropriate to his feeling, Thoreau called the natural world the "face of God," but as a religious thinker, he would not let that energy be reduced to a projection of humanity, to a bearded, white-robed being enthroned above us. It was the mystery concealed in the snowy wood to which his feet would never take him—but toward which love would somehow, eventually, lead him. "Our religion is where our love is." Our religion is here, in this glorious world, in one sense, and in another sense it is not here but in "a place beyond all place," one that we can know only by an inner groping in the dark. I think Thoreau is saying that our love is what unites these outer and inner realms. Perhaps we have to leave the puzzle there.

Acknowledgments

Even in writing a book, many hands make light work. I'm deeply grateful to Larry Buell, Robert Gross, John Buehrens, Christopher Dustin, Mark Harris, Nate Klug, and Rebecca Kneale Gould for reading portions of the manuscript, providing incisive feedback, and sharing their thoughts with me. Jenny Rankin, who is as estimable a scholar as helpmate, was especially generous as well as penetrating in reading the manuscript in all its all stages and encouraging me to keep moving forward.

Thanks to the scholars Paul Schacht of the Digital Thoreau project, Beth Witherell of the Writings of Henry D. Thoreau, David Gordon of Loyola University, Dan McKanan of Harvard Divinity School, Jeff Cramer of the Thoreau Institute at Walden Woods Project, Robert Sattelmeyer, and Anke Voss and Jessie Hopper of Special Collections at the Concord Free Public Library for fielding questions or providing research materials. I was set straight on Puritan thought by David Hall and on dark-green religion by Bron Taylor. Thank you to friends and colleagues including Henrik Otterberg, Barry Andrews,

Chris Walton, Burton Carley, Robert Thorson, Kimberley Patton, Ron Hoag, Lucas Nossaman, John Kaag, Jeff Bilbro, and Wes Mott for discussing the project with me. I especially value my conversations about Thoreau's religion with the late Robert D. Richardson, who remains, as ever, an inspiration. This book would not have been possible without the scholarly contributions of Alan Hodder, Chris Dustin, Laura Walls, David Robinson, Becky Gould, Malcolm Clemens Young, and William Wolf.

Presentations on Thoreau's religious thought that I have given at Harvard Divinity School and Holy Cross College, and at public forums hosted by the Thoreau Society, Thoreau Farm Trust, First Parish in Concord, and local libraries were helpful in clarifying and crystallizing this project. Special thanks to the editors of the Religion Around series at Penn State University Press for helping me formulate this idea as a book.

Finally, heartfelt thanks to the sharp-eyed, incisive, and supportive Kyle Wagner, my editor at the University of Chicago Press, and to the production team at the Press. While these and others I have not named deserve credit for what is good in these pages, any bloopers or omissions are mine alone.

A Note on Sources

Quotations from Thoreau's essays and books are from the scholarly editions prepared by the Writings of Henry D. Thoreau in conjunction with Princeton University Press. His *Journal* quotes are from both *The Journal of Henry David Thoreau*, published in 1906 by Houghton Mifflin in fourteen volumes, and the eight volumes of his *Journal*, up through 1854, published to date by Princeton. While the latter is the scholarly edition of the *Journal*, I use some quotes from the 1906 edition because it is the most widely available and readable edition. (The 1906 passages have been checked for capitalization and accuracy against the Princeton *Journal* volumes in print and the project's transcripts online.) Thoreau wrote rapidly in his *Journal* to get down first impressions, and his spelling and punctuation are uneven. I have occasionally standardized his punctuation for the sake of readability. I give a citation to the Princeton edition in the notes (e.g., PJ 1:61), a date for the 1906 edition (e.g., *Journal*, August 17, 1851). The salient phrase of the quoted material is given in the citation. This includes all quotes in the paragraph unless another cite is given. No note is given if the date of the quoted passage appears in the text.

Abbreviations

Correspondence	Henry David Thoreau. *Correspondence*. Edited by Robert N. Hudspeth, with Elizabeth Witherell and Lihong Xie. 3 vols. Princeton, NJ: Princeton University Press, 2013–2024.
Cape Cod	Henry David Thoreau. *Cape Cod*. Edited by Joseph J. Moldenhauer. Princeton, NJ: Princeton University Press, 1988.
Days	Walter Harding. *The Days of Henry Thoreau: A Biography*. Princeton, NJ: Princeton University Press, 1982.
Ecstatic Witness	Alan D. Hodder. *Thoreau's Ecstatic Witness*. New Haven, CT: Yale University Press, 2001.
EEM	Henry David Thoreau. *Early Essays and Miscellanies*. Edited by Joseph J. Moldenhauer and Edwin Moser, with Alexander C. Kern. Princeton NJ: Princeton University Press, 1975.
Excursions	Henry David Thoreau. *Excursions*. Edited by Joseph J. Moldenhauer. Princeton, NJ: Princeton University Press, 2007.
Journal	Henry David Thoreau. *The Journal of Henry David Thoreau*. 14 vols. Edited by Bradford Torrey and Francis Allen. Boston: Houghton Mifflin, 1906.
Letters	Henry David Thoreau. *Letters to a Spiritual Seeker*. Edited by Bradley P. Dean. New York: W. W. Norton, 2004.
Maine Woods	Henry David Thoreau. *The Maine Woods*. Edited by Joseph J. Moldenhauer. Princeton, NJ: Princeton University Press, 1972.
PJ	Henry David Thoreau. *Journal: The Writings of Henry D. Thoreau*. 8 vols. Edited by John Broderick et al. Princeton, NJ: Princeton University Press, 1981–2002.

Reform Papers	Henry David Thoreau. *Reform Papers*. Edited by Wendell Glick. Princeton, NJ: Princeton University Press, 1973.
Walden	Henry David Thoreau. *Walden*. Edited by J. Lyndon Shanley. Princeton, NJ: Princeton University Press, 1971.
A Week	Henry David Thoreau. *A Week on the Concord and Merrimack Rivers*. Edited by Carl F. Hovde, William L. Howarth, and Elizabeth Witherell. Princeton, NJ: Princeton University Press, 1980.

Notes

Introduction

1. "How do I know," "Life without Principle," in *Reform Papers*, 168.
2. "an ancient and tottering frame," *A Week*, 69; "The church is a sort of hospital," *A Week*, 76.
3. "religion by revelation," Ralph Waldo Emerson, *Nature* (1836; San Francisco: Chandler, 1968), 5; "a newer testament," "Walking," in *Excursions*, 220.
4. "A man's faith," *A Week*, 78.
5. "Without religion," PJ 5, 261.
6. "the feelings, acts, and experiences," James, *Varieties of Religious Experience*, Modern Library (New York: Random House, 1902), 31.
7. "I am pledged to it," PJ 5, 437.
8. "never reasons, never proves," Emerson, *The Selected Letters of Ralph Waldo Emerson*, ed. Joel Myerson (New York: Columbia University Press, 1997), 133; "interior evidence," *A Week*, 292.
9. "at the meeting of two eternities," *Walden*, 17. On the distinction between the sacred and the profane, see Mircea Eliade, *The Myth of the Eternal Return: Cosmos and History* (Princeton, NJ: Princeton University Press, 1971), 5; see also Eliade, *The Sacred and the Profane: The Nature of Religion* (New York: Harper Torchbooks, 1961), 26. Eliade in recent years has been criticized for overgeneralizing on the basis of too little empirical research and for his ties to fascist Romanian organizations in the 1930s, but his fundamental ideas remain influential.

10. "No writer of the present day," John Weiss, *Christian Register*, 1865, reprinted in *Pertaining to Thoreau*, ed. Samuel A. Jones (Boston: Edwin B. Hill, 1901), 147; "If I understand rightly," Blake to Thoreau, March 1848, *Letters*, 34. (No further date is given.) Blake was one of six graduating students (along with faculty and local clergy) present for Emerson's Divinity School Address on July 15, 1836. Here Blake is suggesting that Thoreau is going beyond Emerson's advice in his address to "let the breath of new life be breathed by you through the forms already existing"; "a certain petulance of remark," Ralph Waldo Emerson, "Biographical Sketch," in *The Writings of Henry David Thoreau* (Boston: Houghton Mifflin, 1906), 1:xxxv.

11. "deeply religious," F. B. Sanborn, *Henry D. Thoreau* (Boston: Houghton Mifflin, 1893), 299; "Yes, he was religious," Pratt quoted in Edward Waldo Emerson, *Henry Thoreau as Remembered by a Young Friend* (Toronto: Dover, 1969), 33; "I think Henry was a person," Sophia Thoreau to Daniel Ricketson, February 7, 1863, *Daniel Ricketson and His Friends: Letters, Poems and Sketches* (Boston: Houghton Mifflin, 1902), 155. Emily Lyman wrote a booklet, *Thoreau* (Concord, MA: Patriot Press, 1902), of which only 110 copies were privately printed.

12. "I suppose that I should surprise," Emily Lyman quoted in "'Our Ideal Is the Only Real': Emily R. Lyman on Thoreau's Religion," Thomas Blanding, *Concord Saunterer* 14, no. 2 (Summer 1979): 2.

13. Herbert Wendell Gleason, *Through the Year with Thoreau* (Boston: Houghton Mifflin, 1906), xxxiii.

14. "Fifty years from now," *Days*, 274; "for anyone who could," Barry Lopez, *Horizon* (New York: Knopf, 2019), 43. On Thoreau's religion as a factor in his popularity today, I am indebted to John Buehrens.

15. Although this quote is often attributed to Teilhard, its authenticity is in doubt. An online archive of Teilhard's works notes that it is attributed to him in *The Joy of Kindness* (1993), by Robert J. Furey, 138, as well as by the motivational speaker Wayne Dyer and by Stephen Covey, in *Living the 7 Habits: Stories of Courage and Inspiration* (2000), 47. However, Moira Timms attributes it to G. I. Gurdjieff in *Beyond Prophecies and Predictions: Everyone's Guide To The Coming Changes* (1993), 62. Neither Furey nor Timms give a source. See American Teilhard Association, "Teilhard's Quotes" (n.d.), https://teilharddechardin.org/teilhard-de-chardin/teilhards-quotes/.

16. For an overview of American religious liberalism, see Leigh Schmidt, *Restless Souls* (Princeton NJ: Princeton University Press, 2006).

17. "The ultimate expression or fruit," *Journal*, March 7, 1859.

18. "who had been fishing," *Walden*, 173.

19. "My Friend is not of some other race," *A Week*, 284.
20. "Give me a sentence," *A Week*, 151.
21. On Thoreau's ascetic lifestyle, see Alda Balthrop-Lewis, *Thoreau's Religion: Walden Woods, Social Justice, and the Politics of Asceticism* (Cambridge: Cambridge University Press, 2020), 162–208.
22. "I would fain improve," *Journal*, August 30, 1856.
23. "for my faith and aspiration," Thoreau to Blake, March 27, 1848, *Letters*, 38; "To pray is to take notice," Abraham Joshua Heschel, *Moral Grandeur and Spiritual Audacity: Essays*, ed. Susannah Heschel (New York: Farrar, Straus and Giroux, 1997), 341.

Chapter One

1. "I do not wish," First Parish in Concord Records, 1695–2014, Special Collections, Concord Free Public Library.
2. "I condescended to make," "Civil Disobedience," in *Reform Papers*, 79.
3. "which is never permitted to go out," PJ 1:165.
4. "I will be thankful," *Journal*, January 2, 1852.
5. "We check and repress," *Journal*, November 16, 1851, "The kernel is still," Henry D. Thoreau, *Faith in a Seed*, ed. Bradley P. Dean (Washington, DC: Island Press, 1993), 179.
6. "Every blade in the field," Thoreau to Emerson, March 11, 1842, *Correspondence*, 1:105.
7. Thoreau often wrote quickly in his *Journal* to record fresh impressions and edited later for publication. Since he calls Emerson cold and reserved here, he may have meant to say his love is waning, or declining, not waxing. Alternatively, if Thoreau meant what he wrote, it is possible Emerson acted more coldly when his love waxed because he was trying to control it. In 1838, a year after his friendship with Emerson began, Thoreau's poem, "Friendship," suggests he intuited that Emerson, despite being his soul's companion, would not to be the intimate friend he so desired. It depicts two mighty oaks that grow up side by side in a meadow. Though their roots are intertwined inseparably, their branches barely touch above ground.

Chapter Two

1. Edward Waldo Emerson, *Henry Thoreau as Remembered by a Young Friend* (Toronto: Dover Publications, 1969), 33; F. B. Sanborn, *Henry D. Thoreau* (Boston: Houghton Mifflin, 1893), 49.
2. "Those divine sounds," PJ 1:61.
3. "absolute, pure Morality," Parker, "The Transient and Permanent

in Christianity" (sermon, Boston, May 19, 1841), available at https://
archive.vcu.edu/english/engweb/transcendentalism/authors/parker
/transient.html. For an excellent summary of the origins of American Unitarianism, and the conservative reaction to it, see Alice Blair
Wesley, Peter Hughes, and Frank Carpenter, "The Unitarian Controversy and Its Puritan Roots," https://www.uudb.org/the-unitarian
-controversy/.

4.   Thoreau was descended on his father's side from Huguenots, French
Calvinists who, in order to avoid persecution in Catholic France, at
times hid and worshipped in the forest.

5.   On the religious turmoil in the Thoreau household, see Robert A.
Gross, "Faith in a Boarding House," *Thoreau Society Bulletin*, no.
250, Winter 2005; "majority of one," "Civil Disobedience," in *Reform
Papers*, 74.

6.   "When I was young," *Journal*, April 16, 1852.

7.   "slightly prejudiced," *A Week*, 71; Sabbath school records, First Parish
Church, Special Collections, Concord Free Public Library. On the es-
tablishment of a permanent Sunday school in Concord, see unsigned
article, possibly by Ezra Ripley, "Concord Sabbath School," *Boston
Recorder*, January 30, 1919. On Thoreau's youthful relationship to First
Parish Church, see Laura Dassow Walls, *Henry David Thoreau: A Life*
(Chicago: University of Chicago Press, 2017), 47–49.

8.   On Thoreau's encounter with Brownson, see David Robinson,
Natural Life: Thoreau's Worldly Transcendentalism (Ithaca, NY: Cornell
University Press, 2004), 11–12.

9.   "For every oak and birch," *A Week*, 45.

10.   Robert D. Richardson, "Schleiermacher and the Transcendentalists,"
in *Transient and Permanent: The Transcendentalist Movement and Its
Contexts*, ed. Charles Capper and Conrad Wright (Charlottesville, VA:
University of Virginia Press, 1998), 122–29 and 138; George Behrens,
"Feeling of Absolute Dependence or Absolute Feeling of Depen-
dence?," *Religious Studies*, December 1998, 471–81.

11.   On Thoreau's response to Ellen, see *Days*, 96; "You glance up these
paths," *Journal*, January 30, 1841.

12.   "What have the Concord and Merrimack," quoted in Horace Elisha
Scudder, *James Russell Lowell: A Biography* (Boston: Houghton Mifflin,
1901), 292; "I cannot read a sentence," PJ 1:316; "In the Hindoo scripture," PJ 1:324; "In my brain is the sanscrit," PJ 1:387. On the influence of Asian religions on Thoreau, see *Ecstatic Witness*, 174–217.

13.   "The spontaneous overflow," Wordsworth and Samuel Taylor
Coleridge, *Lyrical Ballads, with Other Poems* (London: T.N. Longman
and O. Rees, 1800), 291; "authentic tidings," Wordsworth, *The Excur-*

sion: A Poem (London: Edward Moxon, 1853), 157. On Wordsworth's influence on Thoreau, see *Ecstatic Witness*, 49–52.

14. "Had he lived," Isaac Hecker, review of Thoreau's *Cape Cod, Catholic World*, November 1865, 283; "the old monks," Laura Dassow Walls, *Henry David Thoreau: A Life* (Chicago: University of Chicago Press, 2017), 241; "I see a kind of real likeness," H. A. Page [Alexander Hay Japp], *Thoreau: His Life and Aims* (London: Chatto and Windus, 1877), ix.

15. "I think *Pilgrim's Progress* is," *A Week*, 71; "rare and delectable places," *Walden*, 88.

16. "Do not we Protestants," *Journal*, October 21, 1859; "have *somewhat hastily* concluded," *Walden*, 91.

17. "I yet lack discernment," *Journal*, November 12, 1837.

Chapter Three

1. "continuously to remind man," "Barbarities," in *EEM*, 109.

2. "I wish I could be as still," PJ 1:349 (December 29, 1841); "What if you or I," PJ 1:373 (March 14, 1842).

3. "The communications from the gods," *Journal*, April 9, 1856.

4. PJ 1:4.

5. "Terror is in all cases," quoted by Thoreau, Harvard essay "Sublimity," in *EEM*, 93. Rudolf Otto, in his classic exploration of the numinous in 1917, also acknowledged this fearful aspect of the holy. It is both a "daunting awfulness and majesty" as well as "something uniquely attractive and fascinating." Otto, *The Idea of the Holy* (Oxford: Oxford University Press, 1923), 31.

6. "The Deity would be reverenced," "Sublimity," in *EEM*, 96; "Yes, that principle," "Sublimity," in *EEM*, 98.

7. "How happens it," *Journal*, August 30, 1856.

8. "I see that all is not garden," *Journal*, August 30, 1856.

9. "With by far the greater part of mankind," "Moral Excellence," in *EEM*, 107.

10. Quotations in the discussion in this section are from *Excursions*, 87–89.

11. On the discussion at the beginning of this section, see Thoreau's "Inspiration," in *Collected Essays and Poems*, ed. Elizabeth Hall Witherell (New York: Library of America 2001), 566.

12. "In the presence of nature," Ralph Waldo Emerson, "The Eye and the Ear" (lecture, December 27, 1837), in *The Early Lectures of Ralph Waldo Emerson*, ed. Stephen Whicher, Robert Spiller, and Wallace Williams (Cambridge, MA: Harvard University Press, 1966–72), 2:274.

13. "neither future nor past," Augustine, *Confessions: Books 9–13*, ed. Carolyn Hammond, Loeb Classical Library (Cambridge, MA: Harvard University Press, 2016), 231; "The foundation of reverence," Alfred North Whitehead, *The Aims of Education* (New York: Simon & Schuster, 1967), 14.

14. "Why does not God," *Journal*, March 25, 1842; "What, then can I do," *Journal*, January 8, 1842.

15. "How munificent is nature," *Journal*, October 16, 1858.

16. "I bend the twig and write my prayers," *Journal*, February 8, 1841; "It is with infinite yearning," *Journal*, August 14, 1854; "Did you ever hear," Thoreau to Blake, March 27, 1848, *Letters*, 37.

17. Cromwell's pocket Bible was printed in London in 1645 in four thin volumes and originally owned by Thomas Belasyse, 1st Viscount Fauconberg. The Latin phrase is inscribed on the flyleaf of the third volume under the stylized initials "O. C." Whether it was Cromwell or a descendent who inscribed the Latin is not certain. The Bible was exhibited an 1848 meeting of the Sussex Archaeological Society of England by a Cromwell descendent, the Earl of Chichester, who asserted that the large *O* and *C* represented Cromwell's signature. For a detailed summary of the provenance of the pocket Bible, see "If I Cease Becoming Better, I Shall Soon Cease To Be Good," *Quote Investigator* (blog), October 27, 2019, www.quoteinvestigator.com /2019/10/27/good-better/; "My desire for knowledge is intermittent," *Journal*, February 9, 1851.

18. "Pursue some path," *Journal*, October 18, 1855.

Chapter Four

1. "The only prayer," PJ 1:188; "easier to live because his aunt," "Life without Principle," in *Reform Papers*, 162; "Truth is high," Guru Nanek quoted in SikhiWiki, "Truth Is High but Higher Still Is Truthful Living" (n.d.), accessed January 2024, https://www.sikhiwiki.org /index.php/Truth_is_high_but_higher_still_is_truthful_living.

2. "For my part," Thoreau to Williams, October 8, 1841, *Correspondence*, 1:88.

3. "The question is not," "Slavery in Massachusetts," in *Reform Papers*, 103.

4. "Now what kind of religion," *Journal*, July 8, 1852; "He is quite alone," *Journal*, August 7, 1853.

5. "The eye has many qualities," PJ 1:375; "Each natural object," PJ 1:281; Thomas Cole, "Essay on American Scenery," *American Monthly Magazine*, January 1836, 12.

6. "Be not preoccupied with looking," *Journal*, September 13, 1852.

7. "To be awake is to be alive," *Walden*, 90; "but when, as it were, by accident," *Journal*, January 4, 1851.
8. "God asks nothing," Loren C. Eiseley, *The Star Thrower* (New York: Houghton Mifflin Harcourt, 1979), 232; Simone Weil, *Gravity and Grace* (New York: Psychology Press, 2002), 117; "I believe that the mind," *Reform Papers*, 173; "a place where three," *Journal*, March 4, 1841.
9. "Life without Principle," in *Reform Papers*, 171.
10. "All the phenomena of nature," PJ 5:159.
11. "inexpressible happiness," *Journal*, December 15, 1841.
12. "Thou openest all my senses," *Journal*, February 20, 1841; "Depend upon that," Thoreau to Blake, November 20, 1849, *Letters*, 50.
13. "the interjections of God," *Journal*, January 8, 1842; "The profane never hear," *Journal*, June 28, 1840.
14. "There are a few sounds," *Journal*, December 30, 1853.
15. "I recover my spirits," *Journal*, August 17, 1851; "Why was it made," *Journal*, January 1, 1852.
16. "the gospel of the wood thrush," *Journal*, June 22, 1853.
17. "It lifts and exhilarates me," *Journal*, June 22, 1853.
18. "solid and sunny earth," *Journal*, March 1, 1852; "beyond the range of sound," *A Week*, 173.
19. "In the broadest and most general," William James, *Varieties of Religious Experience: A Study in Human Nature*, Modern Library (New York: Random House, 1902), 53.
20. "In such a season," *Journal*, January 8, 1842.
21. "I was always conscious of sounds," *Journal*, February 21, 1842.
22. "when we are awake," PJ 1:280.
23. "Though I am old enough," PJ 1:480.
24. "shipwrecked," *Walden*, 326; "We daily live the fate," PJ 4:77. Thoreau also alludes to Moses on Mount Pisgah in his *Journal* on September 7, 1851, and January 24, 1852.
25. "On one side of man," *Journal*, April 3, 1842. Here Thoreau uses *reason* in its more contemporary meaning of rational understanding, in contrast to Emerson and other Transcendentalists, who used it to mean imagination or intuition and thus contrasted Reason and Understanding.
26. For the following discussion on redpolls, see *Journal*, December 11, 1855.

Chapter Five

1. John Weiss, *The Christian Register*, 1865, reprinted in *Pertaining to Thoreau*, ed. Samuel A. Jones (Boston: Edwin B. Hill, 1901), 147.

2. "Historical Introduction," *A Week*, xvi.

3. "The church!," *Journal*, November 16, 1858.

4. Thoreau generally shunned First Parish as an adult but he did go on rare occasions, for example to hear his Harvard professor Henry Ware preach. On Sunday, January 15, 1843, Lidian Jackson Emerson, a faithful churchgoer, wrote her husband that Thoreau had uncharacteristically gone to church that day. "I had a conversation with him a few days since on his heresies," she quipped, "but I had no expectation of so speedy a result." *Correspondence* 1:126.

5. "A temple was anciently," Thoreau to Blake, July 21, 1852, *Letters*, 65; "needs not only to be spiritualized," *A Week*, 379.

6. "There is no infidelity," *A Week*, 76.

7. "The god that is commonly worshipped," *A Week*, 65; "They think they love God!" *Journal*, November 16, 1851.

8. Miller had a nationwide following. His financial backers said they paid for the printing of five million pamphlets. How many of these were distributed is unknown.

9. "There are various, nay," *A Week*, 66.

10. "The Gods are of no sect," PJ 1:301; "The entertaining of a single thought," PJ 5:289; "I perceive no triumphant superiority," PJ 4:98.

11. "less a position on," *Buechner 101: Essays and Sermons by Frederick Buechner*, ed. Anne Lamont (Cambridge: Frederick Buechner Center, 2014), 88; "Father, Son, and Holy Ghost," *A Week*, 70.

12. "The only faith that men recognize," PJ 1:55; "That we have but little faith," Thoreau to Blake, May 2, 1848, *Letters*, 42.

13. "None of the heathen," PJ 1:483.

14. "never reasons, never proves," *The Selected Letters of Ralph Waldo Emerson*, ed. Joel Myerson (New York: Columbia University Press, 1997), 133 (Lawrence Buell and others have noted that Emerson's use of "reason" here diverges from Kant's use of the term to mean intuit or imagine in *The Critique of Pure Reason*); "The soul does not inspect," *Journal*, November 2, 1840.

15. "The destiny of the soul," PJ 1:405.

16. "In the very indistinctness," *A Week*, 152–53.

17. "The wisest man preaches," *A Week*, 70.

18. "but any direct revelation," *Journal*, November 16, 1851; "Our age is retrospective," Emerson, *Nature* (1836; San Francisco: Chandler Publishing, 1968), 5; Emerson as the "mind of the United States," *Henry David Thoreau: Modern Critical Views*, ed. Harold Bloom (New York: Chelsea House, 1987), 1.

19. "How much more religion," *Journal*, January 2, 1853.

20. "rathole revelation," Emerson quoted in Moncure D. Conway, *Emerson at Home and Abroad* (Boston: Osgood, 1882), 189.
21. "Concord is just as idiotic," Thoreau to Sophia Thoreau, July 13, 1852, *Correspondence* 2:113.
22. "I should make haste," Thoreau to Sophia Thoreau, July 13, 1852, *Correspondence* 2:113.
23. "Those faint revelations of the Real," *A Week*, 385.
24. "Men esteem truth remote," *Walden*, 97.
25. "Commonly men live," *Journal*, December 6, 1859.
26. "the vitality and force," "Civil Disobedience," in *Reform Papers*, 63.
27. "They who know of no purer," "Civil Disobedience," in *Reform Papers*, 88.
28. "an ancient tottering frame," *A Week*, 69; "It is like towing a sinking ship," *Journal*, January 1, 1858.
29. "Though every kernel," *Journal*, March 5, 1852.
30. "so truly strange," *A Week*, 72.
31. "Think of repeating," *A Week*, 73.

Chapter Six

1. "Let us have institutions," *Journal*, November 16, 1858; Christianity "has hung its harp," *A Week*, 77.
2. "The underlying foundation of life," Harriet Beecher Stowe, *The Writings of Harriet Beecher Stowe* (Cambridge: Houghton Mifflin, 1897), 10:421.
3. "Now if there are any," *Journal*, February 10, 1852.
4. "to take leave of my sin," *Journal*, February 14, 1851; "A wise man will dispense," PJ 1:61; "One cannot too soon forget," PJ 1:363.
5. "gained from the Stoics," quoted in Mark W. Harris, "Bringing Up the Bodies," *Journal of Unitarian Universalist Studies* 43 (2020): 40; "teaches how to eat," *Walden*, 221.
6. "Every man is the builder," *Walden*, 221.
7. "Though you be a babe," *Journal*, December 20, 1851; "They fill the churches," *Journal*, September 23, 1859.
8. "In the new Adam's rise," PJ 3:187; "We loiter in winter," *Walden*, 314.
9. "Sin, I am sure," *Journal*, December 26, 1841; "Woe be to the generation," *Journal*, December 20, 1851; "a state before it is an act," Paul Tillich, *The Shaking of the Foundations* (New York: Charles Scribner & Sons, 1947), 155.
10. "Last night I treated," *Journal*, December 31, 1851.
11. "obey the hint which God gives them," *Walden*, 315.

12. "The doctrines of despair," "A Natural History of Massachusetts," in *Excursions*, 5; "Our hymn-books," *Walden*, 78.
13. "the funeral of mankind," *Journal*, November 10, 1851; "I think the institution," *Journal*, November 16, 1851.
14. "We are all ordinarily," *Journal*, January 15, 1857.
15. "in a sort of whitewashed prison entry," *Journal*, May 12, 1857.
16. "You must converse," *Journal*, December 30, 1852.
17. "I hear these guns going to-day," *Journal*, January 22, 1859.
18. "I do not know what they mean," *Faith in a Seed*, ed. Bradley P. Dean (Washington, DC: Island Press, 1993), 64.

Chapter Seven

1. "common laws," *Journal*, May 24, 1851; "stings my ear," *Journal*, January 9, 1853.
2. "Our faith comes," Emerson, *The Cambridge Companion to Ralph Waldo Emerson*, ed. Joel Porte (Cambridge: Cambridge University Press, 1999), 116.
3. "My life partakes of infinity," PJ 4:390.
4. "It affected me," PJ 5:439.
5. "of a certain doubleness," *Walden*, 135.
6. "As long as I can remember," *Journal*, July 16, 1851; "sad cheer," *A Week*, 175.
7. "This great expanse," *Journal*, March 12, 1854; "I can remember," PJ 1:400.
8. "I hear the tones," *Journal*, January 24, 1852.
9. "I hear now from Bear Garden Hill," *Journal*, August 5, 1851. This passage refers to the story of Apollo, the Greek god of light, music, and poetry, who, after killing Python, is banished from Mount Olympus and condemned to guard the flocks of King Admetus.
10. "Our most glorious experiences," *Journal*, May 24, 1851; "some victorious melody," Thoreau to Lucy Jackson Brown, January 24, 1843, *Correspondence* 1:119.
11. "In my better hours," *Journal*, July 22, 1851.
12. "I hear one thrumming," *Journal*, January 13, 1857.
13. "A certain tendency," *The Spiritual Emerson: Essential Writings by Ralph Waldo Emerson*, ed. David M. Robinson (Boston: Beacon Press, 2004), 161.
14. "Surely joy is the condition," "The Natural History of Massachusetts," in *Excursions*, 5; joy as a sign of God's presence, William Ockham [pseud.], "Teilhard de Chardin Quote of the Week (May 27): Joy and the Presence of God," *Teilhard de Chardin* (blog), May 27, 2013, https://

teilhard.com/2013/05/27/teilhard-de-chardin-quote-of-the-week-may
-27-joy-and-the-presence-of-god/.

Chapter Eight

1. Lowell's and Greeley's critical judgments are quoted in *Ecstatic Witness*, 132.
2. Bron Taylor, "From the Ground Up: Dark Green Religion and the Environmental Future," in *Ecology and the Environment: Perspectives from the Humanities*, ed. Donald K. Swearer (Cambridge, MA: Harvard University Press, 2008), 89.
3. "see the forms of the mountains," *Journal*, August 14, 1854; "jaundice reflected from man," *Journal*, August 1, 1841.
4. Greeley letter to Thoreau, January 2, 1853, *Correspondence*, 2:145; "since I was born to be a pantheist," Thoreau to Greeley, February 9, 1853, *Correspondence*, 2:153.
5. "most constant" at Pan's shrine, *A Week*, 65; "Pan himself lives in the wood," PJ 1:347.
6. "May we not see God," *A Week*, 382.
7. "not only to be spiritualized," *A Week*, 379.
8. "When the common man," *A Week*, 382.
9. "It is easier to discover," *A Week*, 383.
10. "I am grateful for what I am," Thoreau to Blake, December 6, 1856, *Letters*, 142.
11. "the significance of phenomena," *Journal*, August 5, 1851; "the physical fact which in all language," *Journal*, February 15, 1860. The full quote is "As in the expression of moral truths we admire any closeness to the physical fact which in all language is the symbol of the spiritual, so, finally, when natural objects are described, it is an advantage if words [are] derived originally from nature," insofar as they have been turned "from their primary signification to a moral sense."
12. Actual events "are less far real," Thoreau to Blake, August 9, 1850, *Letters*, 60.
13. "Man cannot afford to be a naturalist," *Journal*, March 23, 1853.
14. "Ah give me pure mind," *Journal*, December 25, 1851.
15. "We soon get through with Nature," *Journal*, May 23, 1854.

Chapter Nine

1. Thoreau to Parker Pillsbury, April 10, 1861, *The Quotable Thoreau*, ed. Jeffrey Cramer (Princeton, NJ: Princeton University Press, 2011), 240.

2. "Universal Intelligence," PJ 7:186; "the spirit itself," "divine mind," PJ
    1:239; "intelligence with some remote horizon," *Walden*, 312; "Nature
    is full of genius," *Journal*, January 5, 1856; "Emersonianism seems to
    let God evaporate," James, *Varieties of Religious Experience*, Modern
    Library (New York: Random House, 1902), 32.
3. "We strive to retain and increase," PJ 1:178; "Nearest to all things,"
    Walden, 134.
4. "As I stand over the insect," *Walden*, 332.
5. "All life is sanctified," A. H. Papp [Alexander Hay Japp] quoted in *Ec-
    static Witness*, 17; "I believe something," Thoreau to Blake, March 27,
    1848, *Letters*, 38.
6. "It is remarkable," *A Week*, 77. There actually was such an earl.
    Francis Henry Egerton, the eighth earl of Bridgewater, endowed a
    series of lectures on the nature of God that were published as books
    between 1833 and 1836.
7. "The perfect God," *A Week*, 70; "but of the true God," PJ 3:16–17.
8. "The divinity is so fleeting," *Journal*, August 28, 1841. According to
    Abraham Joshua Heschel, "The mystery of God is more adequately
    conveyed *via negationis*, in the categories of negative theology, which
    claims that we can never say what He is, we can only say what He
    is not." Heschel relates this to Jewish tradition of Sabbath, a day
    marked by abstention and what is not done. Heschel, *The Sabbath*
    (New York: Farrar, Straus and Giroux, 1951), 15.
9. Psalms 5, 63, 90, 119, 127, and 130 allude to the night watch or the
    watchman who waits to call out the morning light.
10. "The calling of Jonathan Edwards," John Weiss, *Christian Register*,
    1865, reprinted in *Pertaining to Thoreau*, ed. Samuel A. Jones (Boston:
    Edwin B. Hill, 1901), 144; "And as I was walking there," quoted in
    Samuel Miller, *Jonathan Edwards* (New York: Harper & Brothers,
    1902), 18.
11. "There is in my nature," *A Week*, 54; "The Almighty is wild above all,"
    Journal, January 27, 1853; "The most alive," *Excursions*, 203; "a speci-
    men of what God," *Maine Woods*, 71.
12. "Ah, bless the Lord," *Journal*, January 12, 1855; Psalm 104 is a hymn to
    God's creation. It mentions storks, cattle, goats, lions, and creeping
    things in the sea, but no crows or hens.
13. "In God's wilderness lies," quoted in Linnie Marsh Wolfe, *John of the
    Mountains: The Unpublished Journals of John Muir* (Madison: Univer-
    sity of Wisconsin Press, 1938), 317; "Give me a wildness," *Excur-
    sions*, 202.
14. "Generally speaking, a howling wilderness," *Maine Woods*, 219.
15. "What shall we do," *Journal*, November 16, 1850.

16. "the Scene-shifter," *A Week*, 114; "God is a pure act," *The Works of Jonathan Edwards*, ed. Paul Ramsey (New Haven, CT: Yale University Press, 1957), 13:260; Philip F. Gura discusses the influence of Edwards on the Transcendentalists in "From Edwards to Emerson, Revisited," *Journal of Unitarian Universalist History* 38 (2014–15):1–17. On the similarity between Thoreau's thought and process theology, Whitehead wrote: "History discloses two main tendencies in the course of events. One tendency is exemplified in the slow decay of nature. With stealthy inevitableness, there is degradation of energy. The sources of activity sink downward and downward. Their very matter wastes. The other tendency is exemplified by the yearly renewal of nature in the spring. . . . Reason is the self-discipline of the originative element in history." Alfred North Whitehead, *The Function of Reason* (Boston: Beacon Press, 1929), "Introductory Summary."

17. "There seem to be two sides," PJ 1:372 (March 14, 1842; the entry is given as the 13th in the 1906 *Journal*).

18. "On the outside all the life," *Journal*, March 2, 1854; "There is nothing inorganic," *Walden*, 308.

19. "I am affected as if," *Walden*, 306.

20. "A thrumming of piano-strings," *Journal*, August 13, 1852.

21. "If you consider it," *Journal*, December 16, 1840.

Chapter Ten

1. "Let God alone if need be," Thoreau to Blake, April 3, 1850, *Letters*, 53.

2. "great artist," PJ 4:242; "the Maker," *Journal*, April 16, 1856 (capitalized in the online Princeton transcript); "maker of the Universe," PJ 5:284; "the highest," PJ 5:437; "Universal Intelligence," PJ 7:186.

3. "What form of beauty," *Journal*, August 6, 1852.

4. "Thou art a personality," PJ 3:125; "I perceive I am dealt with," PJ 3:306.

5. "I see, smell, taste, hear, feel," *A Week*, 173.

6. "Their owners were coming," *Cape Cod*, 10.

7. "The mariner who makes," *Cape Cod*, 10.

8. "Whatever humanity I might," *Walden*, 211; "I thank God for sorrow," *Journal*, April 3, 1842.

9. "blown on by God's breath," PJ 1:145; "We must securely love," Coleridge quoted in *PJ* 1:279.

10. "Methinks I am getting," Thoreau to Daniel Ricketson, October 16, 1855, *Correspondence*, 2:366; "What you call bareness," *Journal*, December 5, 1856.

11. See Sherad *Osborn, Stray Leaves from an Arctic Journal; or, Eighteen*

Months in the Polar Regions, in Search of Sir John Franklin's Expedition,
in the Years 1850–51 (New York: George P. Putnam, 1852).

12. Quoted in Bradley P. Dean, "An Orthodox Prayer That Thoreau Admired," *Thoreau Society Bulletin*, no. 250 (Winter 2005): 6.
13. "I am struck by the ease," *Journal*, August 27, 1852.
14. "Though in the seasons," PJ 4:51–52.
15. "In all my lectures," Emerson, *The Spiritual Emerson: Essential Writings*, ed. David M. Robinson (Boston: Beacon Press, 2003), 11; "what was oldest," Bloom, ed., *Henry David Thoreau: Modern Critical Views* (New York: Chelsea House, 1987), 8; "the very movement itself of the soul," James, *Varieties of Religious Experience*, Modern Library (New York: Random House, 1902), 454.
16. "cleave to God," Emerson, *The Complete Works of Ralph Waldo Emerson: The Natural History of the Intellect and Other Papers, vol. 12* (Boston: Houghton Mifflin, 1903), 6; "Universal Soul," *A Week*, 126; "the Unnamed," *A Week*, 136; "the Almighty," *A Week*, 71; "the All," *Journal*, February 8, 1857; "the Great spirit," PJ 2:157; "Artist," *Walden*, 306; "Builder," *Walden*, 329; "Benefactor," *Walden*, 332; "my maker," PJ 3:275; "the author and ruler of the universe," *Journal*, August 27, 1852; "the great Master," PJ 4:256; "A great painter," *Journal*, October 6, 1857; "the works of an old master," *Journal*, November 3, 1857; "a parable of the great teacher," PJ 4:468; "Charioteer," PJ 3:111; "the great chemist," PJ 5:89; "the Great Hare," PJ 7:219; "great Assessor," PJ 4:181; "Great Looker," *Walden*, 270; "Great Mower," *A Week*, 35.

Chapter Eleven

1. "In the midst of a gentle rain," *Walden*, 132.
2. "fundamental feature in the spiritual life," James, *Varieties of Religious Experience*, Modern Library (New York: Random House, 1902), 269.
3. "perhaps a purer, more independent," PJ 2:61; "My love is invulnerable," PJ 1:344.
4. "Chaucer's familiar, but innocent," PJ 1:371.
5. "The protestant church," PJ 1:371.
6. "The flowing sail, the running stream," PJ 1:350.
7. The full quote is "All that is not sporting in the field—as hunting & fishing—is of a religious or else love-cracked character," PJ 5:167; "I cannot conceive," *Journal*, January 23, 1858; "what others get by churchgoing," *Journal*, January 8, 1857.
8. "In the street and in society," *Journal*, January 8, 1857.
9. "the old settler and original proprietor," *Walden*, 137.

10. "ruddy and lusty old dame," *Walden*, 137.
11. *Walden* manuscript version A. View the line "God is my father & my friend" at "Walden: Solitude," Digital Thoreau (n.d.), https:// digitalthoreau.org/walden/fluid/text/05.html.
12. "When you travel," Thoreau to Blake, March 27, 1848, *Letters*, 38.
13. "As I walked on the railroad," *Walden*, 202.
14. "Notwithstanding that I regard myself," PJ 1:144; "Sometimes when I compare myself," PJ 2:159.
15. Ralph Waldo Emerson, "Biographical Sketch," in *The Writings of Henry David Thoreau* (Boston: Houghton Mifflin, 1906), 1:xv.
16. "In friendship," PJ 1:99.
17. "I repeatedly find myself drawn," *Journal*, April 3, 1853; "cold and indifferent tone," *Journal*, February 1, 1852; "If I have not succeeded," *Journal*, February 1, 1852.
18. "Between whom there is hearty truth," *A Week*, 268.
19. "It told me by the faintest," *Journal*, September 12, 1851.

Chapter Twelve

1. "It is not necessary," *A Week*, 67; "If Christ should appear," *Journal*, October 19, 1859.
2. "Of course it makes not the least," PJ 3:203.
3. "While they are hurrying off Christ," *Journal*, June 17, 1854.
4. "Christ" is a "sublime actor," *A Week*, 137; "down to earth and to mankind," *A Week*, 136.
5. "So many years and ages," *A Week*, 136.
6. "visited Olympus even," Thoreau to Blake, April 3, 1850, *Letters*, 54.
7. "any son of God," *Reform Papers*, 178; "that God is, not was," Emerson, "Divinity School Address," *The Spiritual Emerson: Essential Writings*, ed. David M. Robinson (Boston: Beacon Press, 2003), 78; "it dwells, with noxious exaggeration," Emerson, "Divinity School Address," 71; Dickinson to Jane Humphrey, *The Letters of Emily Dickinson*, eds. Thomas H. Johnson and Theodora V. Ward (Cambridge, MA: Harvard University Press, 1986), 1:64; David Friedrich Strauss, *The Life of Jesus, Critically Examined*, trans. Marian Evans (London: Chapman and Hall, 1846).
8. "more living and elastic faith," PJ 5:242.
9. "The nation is not Christian," PJ 4:98.
10. "natural laws of genius," *Journal*, February 1, 1852; "Christ was a gentleman," *Journal*, November 30, 1858.
11. "There was a man," *Journal*, November 16, 1851.
12. "Remarkable for its pure morality," *A Week*, 137.

13. "fit their case exactly," *A Week*, 72; "I love this book rarely," *A Week*, 71.
14. "The one thought I had," *Journal*, January 31, 1852.
15. "A government that pretends," *Journal*, October 13, 1859.
16. "Some eighteen hundred years ago," *Journal*, October 20, 1859; "You who pretend," *Journal*, October 11, 1859.
17. "On the day of his translation," *Journal*, December 5, 1859.
18. Louisa May Alcott, *A Sprig of Andromeda* (New York: Pierpont Morgan Library, 1962), 10. Alcott's letter is one of the most beautiful tributes to Thoreau's life. She wrote it to the woman who proposed marriage to Thoreau, Sophia Foord, whose offer he declined emphatically.

Chapter Thirteen

1. "We pluck and eat," *Wild Fruits: Thoreau's Rediscovered Last Manuscript*, ed. Bradley P. Dean (New York: W. W. Norton, 2001), 52.
2. "have been found wanting," *Walden*, 112. On Thoreau's use of the Bible, see Larry R. Long, "The Bible and the Composition of Walden," *Studies in the American Renaissance* (1979): 310–53; John Robert Burns, "Thoreau's Use of the Bible" (PhD diss., University of Notre Dame, 1966); and Donald Ross Jr., "The Bible as Mentioned in Walden," Kouroo Contexture (n.d.), http://www.kouroo.info/kouroo/WALDEN/BibleAll.pdf.
3. "the Book of Books," *A Week*, 144; "Sabbath School Report, 1825–1832," First Parish in Concord records, Special Collections, Concord Free Public Library. Sabbath school was held informally in parishioners' homes prior to 1818.
4. "By a seeming fate," *Walden*, 5; "The love of Nature," *Journal*, October 29, 1857.
5. "These are my sacraments," PJ 3:4; "Sabbath of the affections," "The Commercial Spirit," *EEM*, 117.
6. If we have "desecrated ourselves," *Reform Papers*, 173.
7. "we attain to a wisdom," *Journal*, January 13, 1857 (alluding to Paul, who said the peace of God "passeth all understanding," Philippians 4:7); "These old stumps," *Journal*, October 21, 1857.
8. "return to dust again," "Autumnal Tints," in *Excursions*, 241.
9. "sacred scripture," *Journal*, October 4, 1859; "In the midst of death," *Journal*, October 10, 1859.
10. "a new kind of prayer-book," *Journal*, June 9, 1852; "Will the haymaker," *Journal*, August 19, 1853; "It is no transient love strain," *Journal*, May 23, 1854; "The catechism says," *Journal*, May 1, 1859.
11. "pointedly secular essay," Robert D. Richardson, *Henry Thoreau: A*

Life of the Mind (Berkeley CA: University of California Press, 1986), 226; "It's a newer testament," "Walking," in *Excursions*, 220.

12. "a new fountain of the muses," "Walking," in *Excursions*, 221.
13. "is perfectly symbolical of the path," "Walking," in *Excursions*, 195.
14. "but was looking for an old post-hole," "Walking," in *Excursions*, 191.
15. "Adam in paradise," "Walking," in *Excursions*, 201; "I believe in the meadow," "Walking," in *Excursions*, 202.
16. "When I would recreate myself," "Walking," in *Excursions*, 205.
17. "Than longen folk to go," Chaucer quoted in "Walking," in *Excursions*, 197.
18. "So we saunter to the Holy Land," "Walking," in *Excursions*, 222.
19. On Thoreau's hope to undermine the church's foundation, see *Journal*, December 18, 1856.
20. Walter Harding, *A Thoreau Handbook* (New York: New York University Press, 1959), 106.

Chapter Fourteen

1. "scripture" with its own parallels, Stanley Cavell, *Senses of Walden* (Chicago: University of Chicago Press, 1973), 14; on Thoreau's effort to overturn and revise Christianity, see Cavell, *Senses of Walden*, 111; "a guide to the higher life," *Walden, An Annotated Edition*, ed. Walter Harding (Boston: Houghton Mifflin, 1995), ix; "I discovered Thoreau," Joyce Carol Oates, "The Visionary Art of Henry David Thoreau," *Conjunctions*, no. 29 (1997): 387.
2. "I bathe my intellect," *Walden*, 298; "his second birth," *Walden*, 108.
3. "Walden was dead," *Walden*, 311.
4. "Being superior to physical suffering," *Walden*, 75.
5. "By a seeming fate," *Walden*, 5; "What mean ye," *Walden*, 32. The biblical allusions were compiled by Walter Harding in *Walden: An Annotated Edition* (Boston: Houghton Mifflin, 1995) and Donald Ross Jr. in "The Bible as Mentioned in Walden," Kouroo Contexture (n.d.), http://www.kouroo.info/kouroo/WALDEN/BibleAll.pdf.
6. "inexpressibly begrimed," *Journal*, September 20, 1851; "wonder at the halo," *Walden*, 202; "Verily a good house," PJ 1:157; "intelligence with some remote horizon," *Walden*, 312, "obtained a patent of heaven," *Walden*, 179.
7. "gem of the first water," *Walden*, 179; "cannot come nearer," *Walden*, 193.
8. "As the sun arose," *Walden*, 86.
9. "a religious exercise," *Walden*, 298.
10. "for one true vision," *A Week*, 140.

11. "Both time and place," *Walden*, 87.
12. "very ancient slough," *Walden*, 6; "Some piece of mica," Thoreau to Blake, February 27, 1853, *Letters*, 86.
13. "drive life into a corner," *Walden*, 91, "I wish to meet the vital facts," PJ 2:156; "whether it is of the devil," *Walden*, 91.
14. "All health and success," *Walden*, 78.
15. Thoreau did not want to pay a tax during the Mexican War (1846–48), part of the impetus for which was the admission of Texas as a slave state. Although the poll tax was a local one, Thoreau was making a stand in principle against supporting an immoral government.
16. "The first sparrow of spring!," *Walden*, 311.
17. Thoreau's reported deathbed sayings are recounted in Harding, *Days*, 464–66; and Walls, *Thoreau: A Life*, 498.
18. "How plain that death," Thoreau to Emerson, March 11, 1842, *Correspondence*, 1:104–5.
19. "May not my life in nature," *Journal*, July 19, 1851.
20. "No new life," Thoreau to Blake, March 27, 1848, *Letters*, 36.
21. "I am reassured and reminded," *Journal*, March 23, 1856.
22. "I love to be reminded," PJ 7:120; "that nature is prepared," *Journal*, November 10, 1854.
23. "when the villagers were lighting," *Walden*, 252.

Chapter Fifteen

1. The signboard was a reference to the first message sent across the cable: "Directors of Atlantic Telegraph Company, Great Britain, to Directors in America:—Europe and America are united by telegraph. Glory to God in the highest; on earth peace, good will towards men."
2. "are never communicated," *Walden*, 216; "for our religion is as unpublic," PJ 1:289. In the Divinity School Address, Emerson said: "Historical Christianity has fallen into the error that corrupts all attempts to communicate religion."
3. "In human intercourse," *A Week*, 278.
4. "sunder yourself," Blake to Thoreau, March 1848, *Letters*, 34. (No further date is given.)
5. "Let God alone if need be," Thoreau to Blake, April 3, 1850, *Letters*, 53; "in a sense they are still in the mail," *Letters*, 13.
6. "I parted from my beloved," Thoreau to Blake, September 1852, *Letters*, 72. No further date is given.
7. "There are some things," *A Week*, 278.
8. "but not many words passed," *Walden*, 174.

9. "and yet not voluntarily kept," *Walden*, 17; "The words which express our faith," *Walden*, 325.
10. "Their truth is instantly translated," *Walden*, 325; "All symbols are fluctional," Ralph Waldo Emerson, "The Poet," in *Essays, Second Series*, vol. 3 of *The Complete Works of Ralph Waldo Emerson, Riverside Pocket Edition* (Boston: Houghton Mifflin, 1903), 34.
11. "bubble on her surface," PJ 1:61.
12. "The din of trivialness is silenced," *Journal*, August 2, 1854.
13. "that we may know what communion," PJ 1:61.
14. "As the truest society," *A Week*, 391; "Silence is the communing," PJ: 1:60.
15. "all revelations," PJ 1:63; "Silence *was*, say we," PJ 1:60; "Her infinite din," *A Week*, 392.
16. "It were vain for me," *A Week*, 393.
17. "A man may run on confidently," *A Week*, 393.
18. "I must stand still and listen," *Journal*, January 21, 1853.
19. "As Bonaparte sent out," Thoreau to Blake, August 8, 1854, *Letters*, 105.
20. "Occasionally we rise above," PJ 1:315.

Chapter Sixteen

1. "Our spirits never go," *Journal*, December 15, 1841; "must look through and beyond her," *Journal*, March 23, 1853.
2. "I keep a mountain," Thoreau to Blake, November 16, 1857, *Letters*, 159.
3. "distant shore," *Cape Cod*, 10; "that other world," *A Week* 385; "land of promise," Thoreau to Blake, November 4, 1860, *Letters*, 191; "that other kind of life," *Journal*, June 22, 1851.
4. "This, our respectable daily life," Thoreau to Blake, March 27, 1848, *Letters*, 37.
5. "We are ever dying," PJ 3:95.
6. Emerson did not provide a citation and the quotation does not appear in Thoreau's *Journal*. He may have heard it from Sophia Thoreau or it may have appeared in a letter or piece of writing lost to us.
7. "There too, as everywhere," *Walden*, 270.
8. Epigraph, *A Week*, 3.
9. "portals to other mansions," *A Week*, 377–78.
10. "I am not without hope," *A Week*, 385.
11. "The society which I was made for," *Journal*, July 19, 1851.
12. "Looking through a stately pine grove," *Journal*, October 31, 1850.
13. "Another singular kind of spiritual foot ball," Thoreau to Blake, April 10, 1853, *Letters*, 89.

14. "Let him step to the music," *Walden*, 326.
15. "the basis of all philosophy, poetry and religion," *Journal*, March 1, 1852.
16. "One of little faith," *Journal*, February 1, 1852.
17. "You must love," *Journal*, January 25, 1858; "I may dream of no heaven," *Journal*, March 11, 1856; "Of thee, O earth," *Journal*, November 7, 1851; "The body is not made negligible," Nan Shepherd, *The Living Mountain* (Aberdeen, UK: Aberdeen University Press, 1977), 106.
18. "down to a heaven," *Journal*, July 17, 1854.
19. "The outward is only," Thoreau to Blake, March 27, 1848, *Letters*, 35; "This earth which is spread out," *Journal*, May 23, 1854.
20. "There is only necessary," *A Week*, 383; "Be a Columbus," *Walden*, 321.
21. "distant shore," *Cape Cod*, 10.
22. "When I hear this bell ring," *Journal*, December 26, 1841.
23. For Brownson's influence on Thoreau, see David Robinson, *Natural Life, Thoreau's Worldly Transcendentalism* (Ithaca, NY: Cornell University Press, 2004), 12–13.
24. "I only went out," John Muir, *John of the Mountains: The Unpublished Journals of John Muir*, ed. Linnie Marsh Wolfe (Madison: University of Wisconsin Press, 1938), 439.
25. "The Thaw," in *Thoreau: Collected Essays and Poems*, ed. Elizabeth Hall Witherell (New York: Library of America, 2001), 521.
26. "be seen as a progression," Lawrence Buell, *Henry David Thoreau: Thinking Disobediently* (Oxford: Oxford University Press, 2023), 111.
27. "The fact will one day flower," *Journal*, January 2, 1837; "mere phenomena," *Journal*, April 19, 1854. See also "Autumnal Tints," in *Excursions*, 223–59.
28. "detect the *anima* or soul," *Journal*, November 7, 1843.
29. "We discover that the only spirit," PJ 3:186.
30. "I may say," *Journal*, January 6, 1858.
31. "A rain which is as serene," *Journal*, January 27, 1858.
32. "if men do ever," *Journal*, April 9, 1858.
33. "We must not expect to probe," *Journal*, March 7, 1859.
34. "There is no ripeness," *Wild Fruits: Thoreau's Rediscovered Last Manuscript*, ed. Bradley P. Dean (New York: Norton, 2001), 243.
35. "But if it is required," *Journal*, October 4, 1859.
36. "The crow, flying high," *Journal*, January 30, 1860.
37. Thoreau to Parker Pillsbury, April 10, 1861, *The Quotable Thoreau*, ed. Jeffrey Cramer (Princeton, NJ: Princeton University Press, 2011), 240.
38. "If anything, it suggests," *Ecstatic Witness*, 259; "was still animated by a devotion," Alan Hodder, "Thoreau and the New American

Spirituality," in *Henry David Thoreau in Context*, ed. James S. Finley (Cambridge UK: Cambridge University Press, 2017), 230.

Chapter Seventeen

1. "He stated that he was a Protestant," *Maine Woods*, 182.
2. "earnest reprovers of the age," PJ 2:117; "a born protestant" and "a protestant *à outrance*," Emerson, "Biographical Sketch," *The Writings of Henry David Thoreau* (Boston: Houghton Mifflin, 1906), vol. 1, xvi–xvii.
3. "There are from time to time," *Journal*, January 26, 1853.
4. "the spiritualizing effect," John Weiss, *Christian Register*, 1865, reprinted in *Pertaining to Thoreau*, ed. Samuel A. Jones (Edwin B. Hill, 1901), 144; "for the love," *A Week*, 67; "The religion I love," PJ 1:289.
5. "No sentiment is so rare," PJ 3:371; "It is the love of virtue," PJ 3:312.
6. "All that a man has to say," PJ 8:98.
7. "What if I feel," *Journal*, June 10, 1855; "Our life without love," *Journal*, March 25, 1842.
8. Thoreau to Williams, September 8, 1841, *Correspondence* 1:89; "Is our life innocent enough," PJ 8:161.
9. "many are the travelers," *Walden*, 17.
10. "It is not that we love," Thoreau to Blake, May 21, 1856, *Letters*, 136.
11. "to stand in true relation," *A Week*, 268.
12. "Inspiration," *Thoreau: Collected Essays and Poems*, ed. Elizabeth Hall Witherell (New York: Library of America, 2001), 566.
13. "very atoms bloom," *Journal*, September 4, 1851.
14. "Does not all this amount," *Journal*, January 1, 1854.
15. "of the Great Hare," *Journal*, January 1, 1854.
16. "Are there not hunters," *Journal*, January 1, 1854.
17. "The value of a religious," Simone Weil quoted in Richard Bell, *Simone Weil: The Way of Justice as Compassion* (New York: Rowman & Littlefield, 1998), 97.
18. Thoreau to Williams, September 8, 1841, *Correspondence* 1:89.

Index